Teaching and Managing Schools

Leadership skills in education management

Other titles in this series

The Head Teacher in the 21st Century
Being a successful school leader
by Frank Green

Mastering Deputy Headship
Acquiring the skills for future leadership
by Trevor Kerry

The Special Educational Needs Coordinator
Maximising your potential
by Vic Shuttleworth

Effective Classroom Teacher
Developing the skills you need in today's classroom
by Trevor Kerry and Mandy Wilding

Performance Management in Schools
Unlocking your team potential
by Susan Tranter and Adrian Percival

Middle Leadership in Schools
Harmonising leadership and learning
by Sonia Blandford

Teaching and Managing in Schools

The Next Step

Susan Tranter

PEARSON
Longman

Harlow, England • London • New York • Boston • San Francisco • Toronto
Sydney • Tokyo • Singapore • Hong Kong • Seoul • Taipei • New Delhi
Cape Town • Madrid • Mexico City • Amsterdam • Munich • Paris • Milan

PEARSON EDUCATION LIMITED

Edinburgh Gate
Harlow CM20 2JE
Tel: +44 (0)1279 623623
Fax: +44 (0)1279 431059
Website: www.pearsoned.co.uk

First published as *From Teacher to Middle Manager* 2000
This second edition published in Great Britain as *Teaching and Managing in Schools* 2006

ISBN-13: 978-0-273-70658-8
ISBN-10: 0-273-70658-6

British Library Cataloguing-in-Publication Data
A catalogue record for this book is available from the British Library

Library of Congress Cataloging-in-Publication Data
Tranter, Susan.
  Teaching and managing in schools : the next step / Susan Tranter.
    p. cm. — (Leadership skills in education management)
  Includes bibliographical references and index.
  ISBN-13: 978–0–273–70658–8 (alk. paper)
  ISBN-10: (invalid) 0–273–70658–8 (alk. paper)
    1. School management and organization.   2. Middle managers.   I. Title.   II. Leadership
skills in education management series.

LB2805.T655 2006
371.1'06—dc22

                                                                                    2006041628

10 9 8 7 6 5 4 3 2 1
10 09 08 07 06

Typeset in 10.5/14pt Latin725BT by 35
Printed and bound in Malaysia

The publisher's policy is to use paper manufactured from sustainable forests.

SUSAN TRANTER is Head of Fitzharrys School in Abingdon, Oxfordshire – a specialist technology college. Previously Susan was associate Headteacher of Matthew Arnold School. During this time Matthew Arnold was one of the most improved schools nationally and was one of the first designated specialist science colleges. Susan has worked as a consultant school leader in a school of concern; a secondment that helped to raise attainment, improve curriculum monitoring and provided leadership consultancy to members of the leadership team.

Susan has worked in a range of secondary schools including single sex, grammar, secondary modern and comprehensive. Susan is author of a number of books and articles including *From Teacher to Middle Manager* (Pearson, 2000) and *Diary of a Deputy* (Routledge, 2002), *How to Run your School, Successfully* (Continuum, 2004) and *Performance Management in Schools* (Pearson, 2006). Susan is a research associate for the NCSL having researched top talent programmes and performance management – her 'Hotseat' was one of the most popular to date with nearly 6000 'hits'. Susan was a guest speaker at the NCSL's Leading Edge conference on Growing Leadership Potential and at the SST/SHA conference on Personalised Learning. Susan wrote a paper for the iNET conference on the Student Voice in education. Having piloted a leadership development course for the Specialist Schools Trust (SST), she was commissioned to produce a series of Teach and Learn Units in collaboration between the SST, BBC and Open University. Susan is currently cohort leader for the Specialist Schools Trust 'Developing Leaders' programme and is a Board member of the TDA.

Contents

List of tasks

List of tables

List of figures

Publisher's acknowledgements

We are grateful to the following for their permission to reproduce copyright material:

Screenshot from the Specialist Schools and Academies Trust schools network website used with permission; Figure 8.1 reproduced with permission from Professor David Hopkins.

In some instances we have been unable to trace the owners of copyright material, and we would appreciate any information that would enable us to do so.

Change and being part of it

– acquiring the skills and experiences to lead

Introduction

Schools and teachers are being affected more and more by the demands and contingencies of an increasingly complex and fast-paced post-modern world. . . . Schools and teachers either cling to bureaucratic solutions . . . more systems, more hierarchies, more laid on change, more of the same.

Hargreaves (1994) describes a world in which there is so much change and the teachers' response to it is either to create more systems and procedures or to retreat into a form of nostalgia. Perhaps this says something to you, the reader, about how you feel about change. Perhaps you have read this quotation and don't really understand the point that is being made because for you it represents neither your vision nor your reality of school. What is it like to be a teacher? Why do people want to be teachers? How is the leader of a department or group of others going to change? Is there a need for leaders in our schools or is this another retreat into some twentieth century thinking? In this opening chapter we begin by exploring these ideas and thinking about what is needed, why we might want to lead a group of professionals and the skills and experiences to be acquired.

At their best, schools are exciting and vibrant places where nothing ever stays the same. This is their appeal. The average sized secondary school will have some 1000 pupils aged 11–18 and about 55 teachers who, together with the secretarial staff, office staff, bursar, site staff, catering teams, librarian, teaching assistants, reprographics technicians and science technicians, will bring the establishment figure up to over 1100.

This chapter isn't about how to run a school – if you are interested in reading about this then we can recommend Percival and Tranter (2004) for a detailed guide to the theory and practice of school leadership at its most senior level. This chapter, and indeed this book, is about leadership and management of departments, year teams and the many groups that are formed in our schools.

Schools should be exciting, vibrant places because they are filled with children who are experiencing education for the first time. While *we* may have taught simultaneous equations or Macbeth or climatology several times, for the *children* in our classes it is the first, and may be the only time they will ever grapple with the algebra, read the play or experience the pain and the pleasure of understanding why a hurricane happens.

Schools are complex and complicated places as well. They are complex because learning cannot be defined and delineated by lesson bells and subject differences. Children learn many things during their time at school – they learn about social responsibility, class divisions, success and failure, fairness and injustice. The rough and tumble of a school day is part of the essential experience of growing up. Schools are places where children play together, work together, learn together, fall out and make up together. Schools are places where children get on with adults, and fall out with adults. They are places where children speak to adults inappropriately, and where adults speak to children and one another in ways that defy the normal boundaries of social interaction. Schools are complicated places because the business of organising the school – so that the timetable works, so that there are teachers in classrooms ready to teach children, so that there are meals ready at lunchtime, and so on – means that the business of organisation is a complicated one.

Above all, schools are learning places. If children do not learn at school then they are failing and pointless places – they are failing the children. Schools consume huge amounts of public money being the primary activity for people aged 5–18 and dominate the lives of parents while their children are at school. If children are happy and successful at school, parents are happy; if children are unhappy or unsuccessful, parents are unhappy. Within this social construct, schools are highly accountable for the outcomes, are set targets and are subject to public scrutiny – why? Because they are responsible for the next generation's education. Education is the force that brings about improvement – without education the world would be without its doctors, lawyers, priests, scientists and so on. As the demands on society increase still further, the demands on our education system will continue to increase. As we become increasingly knowledgeable about the way people learn and the efficacy of teaching, the possibilities and potential of our schools increase exponentially.

Do we need leaders at all? Could we have a school without any leaders? Could we have a community of teachers who simply teach what they think the children in their class need to know? And could those classes be composed only of those who want to be there and need to learn what is being taught? We live in a society in which children are compelled to go to school, and therefore there will always need to be some form of organisation to accommodate the needs of large numbers of people in one institution. Bowring-Carr and West-Burnham (1997) give us a picture of tomorrow's school describing a personalised education system where children have individual education plans, monitored by a personal tutor, and attend various sessions at school at various times of the day. So where does that leave us – where is the certainty that what is being done is right? And where is the future heading?

In the Woody Allen film *Sleeper*, the character wakes up after a sleep of 200 years and finds that all the things that were thought bad for us turn out to be good for us. Is this what will happen to our curriculum in 2206? Will the educators of tomorrow's tomorrow find themselves bemused at our curriculum and the way in which children were made to learn? Perhaps another way of thinking is to ask ourselves, is the school of today modelled on what teachers themselves needed or what the learners of today need? Our education system is organised around what teachers do, but does this compromise what children need? The debate on teaching and learning (or learning and teaching as some would have it) has perhaps been hijacked by a misguided notion of modularisation and personalisation to the exclusion of justification. If we are going to think about the curriculum for the future then we need to be clear on the essential purpose and function of learning.

Organising schooling so that each individual learns at an appropriate rate is predicated on a notion of how children work – indeed on some notion of the human condition. It presumes that every individual is motivated to work, that every child wants to learn, and that if conditions are right then they will. Schooling is anathema to intrinsic motivation. Of course, for some it is the case – there are children who join our schools full of enthusiasm and interest who, when fed the diet of exercises, classwork, homework, chalk and talk, lose the sparkle. There are also those who join our schools with antipathy and antagonism towards what schooling has to offer and flourish as the result of expert teaching. Education – the prize of learning – is what schooling has to offer.

For learning is a social activity. Most of us have experienced the deeper understanding that comes with having to explain to another. One of the real triumphs of the *Assessment for Learning* project has been the importance placed on students explaining to others, looking critically at the work of others – peer assessment has brought about real progress in learning. Watch a group of children skilled in peer assessment and you will see very high levels of understanding and motivation. Their understanding of the material is deep because they have had to learn alongside others, and their knowledge is richer as a result of the collaboration their teacher has led.

It would be nice to think that everyone was motivated to learn – that the individual's frame of reference was entirely based on the need and desire to succeed. Most contributors to the education debate are the product of competitive examinations. For many of us our motivation came from wanting to succeed, not wanting to fail. We secured our places at university because we did better than others. The price that society pays for this level of competition is that we lose so many students who don't enjoy the opportunity that success in public examinations brings. Does the necessity of a system that selects the best and most able for the demands of medicine, law and technology really result in an educational waste-land of failure? Or is the liberalisation of the public examination system an inability to acknowledge that we thrive on competition and extrinsic reward.

So we have a system that is based on linearity and competition. The curriculum we offer is vilified because it is delivered in a linear fashion, and success is determined by public examinations. Do any of us know what the curriculum of 2206 will look like? What will it be like in the year 2206? Will knowledge still matter or will the ability to learn be more important? Is being learned important now? Perhaps learning will be assessed in different ways in 2206 – and perhaps people will take exam-inations or tests at different times and the traditional June examinations will have been replaced by something else. But learning – the ability to apply knowledge to new situations, to have deep understanding of con-cepts, to discriminate between a description and an explanation – will be just as important then as it is today. The school, with the actions of a skilled teacher, is the context for such skills to be developed.

This debate, therefore, is not about the fitness of the current curric-ulum – it is how and what it seeks to bring about and the curriculum itself. It seeks to bring about learning through a variety of means – the social and collaborative act of learning together, of having one's understanding tested out though interaction, the discipline of having to know things in preparation for some form of assessment, the disapproval of another if one doesn't and the joy of success when one does.

Who can decide if integral calculus, the War of the Roses, mole equa-tions or *Hamlet* are 'relevant'. School curricula have evolved over time – some of us learnt about matrices in the sixth form at school, taught about them in the early nineties to GCSE classes, but haven't done so since. Is the mathematics curriculum poorer as a result of this evolution? No, because the ability to use and apply mathematics has been strengthened through a focus on investigation. Learning mathematics has changed because the need to create, use and apply mathematics has become more important than the unthinking application of techniques and processes. The pro-cesses themselves are still important.

If we disassemble our traditional school structures because we think they are bad for us, will we find out in 2206 that being taught together was really a good thing. If we replace all the competitive examinations and assessment procedures because we think that learning doesn't happen in that harshly defined way then will we find out in 2206 that competition brings out the best in people and enables us to select the best for the jobs that have to be done? If we liberalise the education system and let those who teach decide what to do, how and when to assess it, then will we find out in 2206 that those who benefit most from the system deny educational opportunity to those who could benefit more? If we take the immense benefits that the discussion on teaching and learning bring and how we personalise learning for students focusing on making that the universal experience for all, I think we will find, in 2206, that our curriculum has evolved. We will need flexibility because people differ – we will have to be smarter in our approach because learning isn't a linear process and doesn't stop at 16. If we can free ourselves from structural debate and home in on standards then we will find out that the evolution to 2206 will result in a curriculum that is fit for purpose because it has resisted attempts to polarise it into a different debate.

There was a time when being a head of department meant organising the textbooks, doing the orders – and that was pretty much it. The administration tasks for many have been removed, or will be in the future, to enable the subject leader to focus on teaching and learning and leading the group. In many schools the group comprises teachers, technicians, classroom assistants and demonstration staff. Large departments in some of our bigger secondary schools will have over twenty people to be led by the head of department.

Leadership at this level is about teaching and learning first and foremost. It is also about personnel management, budgeting, health and safety, and premises. The job has changed and the influence of school self-evaluation has led to a growing emphasis at this level on the ability to analyse performance and target interventions. Teaching and learning is becoming smarter – the most successful schools are those that identify patterns of progress, target resources and interventions, and analyse the effectiveness of what they have done, and also plan the future on the basis of this evaluation.

The business and practice of education is subject to continuous and continual change. The leaders of the future will be needed to articulate a vision to gather people together and to ensure that the potential of the nation's children is realised. At the department level this is not about organising textbooks (but will include managing the person who does organise the textbooks or other resources) but about being the lead practitioner, the person who understands the subject, its pedagogy and the assessment of learning. It starts with a vision of the subject, a deep understanding of why the subject matters, how children learn and the best way for it to be taught.

If you are going to succeed, the first step is to become an excellent teacher. There are several elements – the OfSTED criteria form a useful benchmark with the skill of differentiation being very important to acquire. In the next section we suggest some techniques.

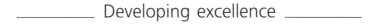 Developing excellence

One way of identifying the qualities displayed by a teacher who is described as 'excellent', is by referring to the OfSTED documents on this subject. Although the nature and methodology of OfSTED inspections is changing – taking account of increased self-evaluation and the National Strategies School Improvement Partners that will be an integral part of the inspection and school improvement process – the OfSTED framework provides a very good benchmark for the quality of teaching, judged in terms of its impact on learning and what makes it successful or not. There are a number of other features which the framework includes:

- the quality of teaching
- how well pupils learn
- how well pupils and students make progress – highlighting relative strengths and weaknesses in English language and literacy, mathematics, particular subjects and stages that help explain pupils' achievement.

These are judgements and evaluations based on the quality of teaching and learning. The central question is, 'How well are pupils or students taught?' However, in seeking to make this evaluation, OfSTED uses a number of criteria which are relevant to the developing teacher. In determining their judgements, inspectors consider the extent to which teachers:

- show good command of areas of learning and subjects
- plan effectively, with clear learning objectives and suitable teaching strategies
- interest, encourage and engage pupils
- challenge pupils, expecting the most of them

- use methods and resources that enable pupils to learn effectively
- make effective use of time and insist on high standards of behaviour
- make effective use of teaching assistants and other support
- where appropriate, use homework effectively to reinforce and extend what is learned in school
- promote equality of opportunity.

This is a long list and the next part of the chapter reflects on the idea of a good teacher and how this has changed over time.

TASK 1

Developing subject knowledge

In this first task, we reflect on the nature of subject knowledge and how teachers demonstrate good subject knowledge and understanding.

1 How do teachers show good subject knowledge and understanding in the way they present and discuss their subjects?

2 In relation to your own subject:

- what elements make up the subject?
- what are the future developments of the subject?
- what are the particular difficulties associated with the teaching of the subject?

Applebee (1989) discusses the nature of teaching as scholarship. He reflects on the image of the necessary preparation for teaching as stressing the importance of knowledge of content – e.g. in the case of an English teacher, of literature. On the face of it, arguments for the importance of such knowledge are unassailable; we can hardly teach a subject we do not know about. The issue here is of a different nature, it concerns the role of such knowledge in school teaching.

However, in the example of language studies Applebee reflects on the past 20 years as having been particularly fruitful, as they have been for the study of child development in general. The theories of Piaget, Vygotsky, Bruner and others have become widely known, and with them emerged the image of a child as an active participant in the process of construction of knowledge. Approaches to reading instruction, for example, were transformed as teachers and scholars became aware of the complex processes of comprehension and understanding that go into a reader's or writer's approach to text. Rather than focusing on the accuracy of the final product, process-oriented approaches to instruction have sought to provide support for the young learner still in the process of solving the problems posed by a particular reading or writing task.

As in language studies we have learned more about the processes of language and learning, we have been developing a third body of knowledge to compete with generic teaching skills and traditional subject scholarship for a place in the teacher–education curriculum. This body of knowledge is *subject-specific knowledge of teaching*. In the case of English teaching, this subject-specific knowledge is based on scholarship in a variety of fields, but the form it takes is different. In its most useful form, the subject-specific knowledge of English teaching is practical knowledge of the nature of children's English skills, the directions of growth these skills will follow, and the contexts that foster such growth. As an example Applebee gives knowledge of the kinds of literature that 12 year olds are likely to find difficult, how they make sense of specific works when they read them, and how teachers can structure classroom activities to develop new skills and strategies that may make initially difficult works accessible.

In this form, subject-specific knowledge of teaching looks very different from knowledge of a traditional subject matter. The concerns of the scholar – whether those focus on the theories of literary criticism or structure of language – are different from the concerns of the classroom teacher. Bennett (1987) thinks that the characterisation of knowledge is difficult methodologically and attempts to represent it by semantic and planning networks and flowcharts. However, the heavy demands made on teachers' knowledge structures to select and set tasks, diagnose pupil conceptions, teach cognitive processes and to manipulate complex learning environments for classes of children requires many of a teacher's actions to become routine. These routine actions simplify the complexity of the teaching task and reduce the cognitive load ensuring the teacher can pay more attention to the substantive activities and goals of teaching.

Past ideas of a 'good teacher'

The notion of the good teacher has changed over time. Successive policies have offered very different, even contradictory, expectations of teachers. Proposals from governments, OfSTED, reform groups or professional associations have often had different, even diametrically opposed, images of the teachers required to carry out their proposals. Teachers working within ensuing projects will have developed skills, knowledge and even career choices which differentiate their idea of a 'good teacher' from that of their colleagues.

An early example of a curriculum statement which describes a strongly enhanced version of the teacher and the curriculum, often referred to by curriculum historians because of its actual or symbolic influence over teachers' work, is contained in the *Handbook of Suggestions for Teachers*. The handbook was produced, and then revised several times during the course of the last century, by the Board, or Ministry, of Education from 1904 right through to the version called *Primary Education* in 1959. Although the handbook contained detailed arguments for curriculum practice and teachers were expected always to have a copy within reach, the preface implied a more liberal, even liberated view of 'the good teacher'.

The only uniformity of practice that the Board of Education desires to see in the teaching of Public Elementary schools is that each teacher shall think for himself and work out for himself such methods of teaching as may use his powers to the best advantage and be best suited to the particular needs and conditions of the school . . . freedom implies a corresponding responsibility in its use.

The strength of the statement should really be judged against the common view of the elementary school teacher which prevailed in the early decades of the twentieth century, which may be characterised as underpaid drudgery performed by poorly educated men and women of low social status. Yet 'good teachers' are now seen as individuals who think about and define their practice in relation to local conditions while recognising their responsibility in relation to the government.

Skilbeck (1989) suggested that the good teacher was characterised as follows.

- The teacher's pedagogical practice will be an area of *that individual's* skill and decision making.

- Pedagogy and content will be updated regularly to ensure improvement in several areas of the curriculum (learning skills, standards, morality etc.). Updating will occur through regular guidelines and directions in the curriculum.

- Assessment in the classroom will be a new skill area to be mastered by teachers who will in turn need to know about the performance indicators applied to them.

- The teacher will recognise the sensitivity of their work in the public and political context, and will need to explain themselves and to negotiate/consult with parents and other sections of the community and to make their curriculum link with the work place and the community.

- The teacher will operate within flexible staffing structures to allow for changes of national priority and economic stringency.

- 'Good teachers' will work within their classrooms and schools on the effective implementation of national curriculum guidelines by means of improved pedagogy, regular knowledge-base updating and the new techniques of assessment. 'Good teachers' will recognise that they work in an education service that has a concentration of control and policy and that it is their duty to work efficiently within national guidelines and to consult local parents, employers and other community members.

Cohen and Manion (1977) describe successful teachers as those who reflected the following elements in their teaching.

- They varied their classroom role from dominative to supportive spontaneously and were able to secure both the students' compliance and initiative as the situation demanded.

- They could switch at will from one role to another and did not blindly follow a single approach to the exclusion of others.

- They were able to move easily from diagnosing a classroom problem to suggesting a follow-up course of action.

- They were able to be both critical of their students and sensitive to their needs as human beings.

Briefly, successful teachers are flexible in their teaching styles and can shift easily and naturally from the direct to the indirect, from being critical observers to sympathetic counsellors, depending on the need.

The perceptual differences between good and poor teachers investigated by Combs (1965) suggest that good teachers can be distinguished from poor ones with respect to the following perceptions about other people.

- Good teachers are more likely to have an internal rather than an external frame of reference. That is, they seek to understand how things seem to others and then use this as a guide for their own behaviour.

- Good teachers are more concerned with people and their reactions than with things and events.

- Good teachers are more concerned with the subjective perceptual experience of people than with objective events. They are, again, more concerned with how things seem to people than just the so-called or alleged facts.

- Good teachers seek to understand the causes of people's behaviours in terms of their current thinking, feelings, beliefs and understandings rather than in terms of forces exerted on them now or in the past.

- Good teachers generally trust other people and perceive them as having the capacity to solve their own problems.

- Good teachers see others as being friendly and enhancing rather than hostile or threatening.

- Good teachers tend to see other people as being of worth. They show regard for a person's dignity and integrity.

- Good teachers see people as their behaviours and essentially developing from within rather than as a product of external events to be moulded or directed. In other words, they were able to be both critical of their class pupils and sensitive to their needs as human beings.

Good teachers bring about effective learning

More particularly, MacGilchrist, Myers and Reed (1997) take a view that the effectiveness of teaching is defined in terms of the learning that takes place. For school learning to be enhanced and effective they argue that teachers need to understand the different factors that can influence a pupil's motivation and ability to learn. To do this, they suggest, that teachers need to be:

- knowledgeable about learning as a process
- knowledgeable about learners
- knowledgeable about what learners want.

One feature which distinguishes new ways of thinking about the effectiveness of the learning process is the focus of attention on the learners themselves. MacGilchrist et al. argue that learners are vital to the learning process. This, at first reading, seems an obvious point.

Bowring-Carr and West-Burnham (1997) discuss the need for schools to change as organisations. The school that they describe is a place where learning is at the centre of the organisation – it is not a school coming from science fiction, but one which is not too far from what some schools are striving towards today. They suggest that there needs to be more thinking on the schools of the future. One aspect of our system and its reluctance to change is the number of teachers who ask that there be no more change for a while. They are suffering, so they claim, from an excess of change and suggest that they are given time for all the upheavals of the last few years to bed down and become routine. There is, Bowring-Carr and West-Burnham argue, no such option. In a world of stability, or at least one of gradual and predictable change, it might have been possible for an institution to remain static and survive. In this world of ever increasing quantitative change, occurring at increasing speed, schools (and therefore teachers) have a stark choice. They can either change, adapting themselves to the new demands and expectations of their students, or not change, and therefore decline in credibility, usefulness and relevance.

The focus of this chapter is to identify those features of a teacher's work which make for excellence.

Quality of teaching – lesson observation

Table 1.1 gives a checklist of the criteria used by OfSTED when assessing quality of teaching.

TABLE 1.1   OfSTED criteria for assessing the quality of teaching

Context of observation

Include:

- a brief description of what the teachers and pupils are doing;
- a brief summary of the lesson content, activities and organisation; and
- describe the role of any support staff and/or other adults present.

Evidence

Teaching – consider the extent to which teachers:

- show good subject knowledge and understanding in the way they present and discuss their subject
- are technically competent in teaching basic skills
- plan effectively, setting clear objectives that pupils understand
- challenge and inspire pupils, expecting the most of them, so as to deepen their knowledge and understanding
- use methods which enable pupils to learn effectively
- manage pupils well and insist on high standards of behaviour

TABLE 1.1   *(cont'd)*

- use time, support staff and other resources, especially ICT, effectively
- assess pupils' work thoroughly and use assessments to help and encourage pupils to overcome difficulties
- use homework effectively to reinforce and/or extend what is learned at school.

Learning – consider the extent to which pupils:

- acquire new knowledge and skills, develop ideas and increase their understanding
- apply intellectual, physical or creative effort in their work
- are productive and work at a good pace
- show interest in their work, are able to sustain their concentration, and think and learn for themselves
- understand what they are doing, how well they have done and how they can improve.

Attainment – consider, for the subject:

- what pupils know, do and understand in the different aspects of the subject
- pupils' understanding and ability to apply their knowledge to related problems
- the extent to which pupils' achievements meet or exceed the levels set by the National Curriculum and, where applicable, the local agreed syllabus for religious education, and any examination or assessment objectives
- any differences in the standards achieved by pupils of different gender or ethnic background
- whether pupils with SEN, those having English as an additional language or those who are gifted and talented, are making good enough progress
- whether standards for the various groups of pupils are high enough.

Attitudes and behaviour – consider the extent to which pupils:

- are keen and eager, and respond well to the educational demands made on them
- behave well in lessons and are courteous, trustworthy and show respect for property
- form constructive relationships with one another, and with teachers and other adults
- work in an atmosphere free from oppressive behaviour such as bullying, sexism and racism

TABLE 1.1 *(cont'd)*

- reflect on what they do and understand its impact on others
- respect other people's differences, particularly their feelings, values and beliefs
- show initiative and are willing to take responsibility.

Any other significant evidence – look for:

- competence in applying skills of literacy, numeracy and ICT
- any effects of staffing, resources or accommodation that impact significantly on standards and quality of work
- other issues relating to SEN, including effectiveness of support staff.

The purpose of this chapter is not to offer detailed guidance on how to become a better teacher – there are countless books which seek to do this. However, an awareness of those criteria which are judged to make one an excellent teacher is essential for the aspiring middle manager. Middle managers who are subject leaders are responsible for the quality of teaching of their subject. Middle managers who are responsible for a Key Stage or a Year group will have their responsibility defined in terms of the achievement of the group. Therefore middle managers, whatever their role, need to have a depth of understanding when considering the issues which affect the quality of teaching and learning.

An important aspect of the teacher's role, which is identified a number of times in the OfSTED criteria, is the role of support staff and other adults. The emphasis on social inclusion and the reduction in the number of special school places have brought this issue to the fore. In developing teaching skill the emphasis placed on the learning needs of students is clearly paramount.

Differentiation

Differentiation is a perennial challenge for all teachers. Bowring-Carr and West-Burnham (1997) describe the need for confidence in the fact that every individual is learning as being a key factor. If the teaching received by students is to be described as being of good quality then, they argue, it has to be 'bespoke'. However, choice is severely constrained in schools – therefore, effective learning requires choice in *how* pupils learn rather than *what* they learn. A first step is to identify the variables of learning that have to be managed. Bowring-Carr and West-Burnham's list of variables is as follows:

- learning styles
- teaching strategies
- prior knowledge
- cognitive skills
- social skills
- feedback, recognition and reinforcement
- neurological factors
- health and diet
- access to resources
- intrinsic motivation
- multiple intelligences
- information technology.

This is a long list and it underlines the increasingly complex role that the teacher has to try to fulfil. Chapter 5 of Bowring-Carr and West-Burnham (1997) is recommended as further reading on this important topic. However, there are particular features of this list that are to be explored in the context of differentiated learning.

TASK 2

Preparing to differentiate a topic

In this task you are asked to consider what constitutes differentiated work in your subject area, and how you can create a 'bespoke' lesson.

Think of a topic that you know well and have taught to a class recently. Think of a class you know well. Identify five students across the ability range in that class (if it is a set, the issue is still pertinent). Identify the different elements of the topic.

- What are the learning outcomes for this topic?
- What prior knowledge did you assume?
- What was your starting point for the topic?
- What assessment did you plan for this topic and at what stage did it inform your planning?

There are some challenging issues to discuss in this activity and we take them in turn.

The ability to identify the different elements of a topic is a critical factor when planning a teaching programme. The effective teacher needs to be able to break the topic down into a range of learning units. Table 1.2 illustrates the way in which a French teacher breaks down the topic of food for a Year 8 class.

What the table illustrates is that by breaking the topic down into a number of elements, the teacher is able to plan a learning programme for pupils. The noteworthy feature of this method is that it identifies at the start what the student has to be able to do by the end of the unit of work. This is important because it enables the teacher to plan the teaching

TABLE 1.2 Topic analysis: skills, outcomes, methods

Topic: Food and Drink

Skills	Outcomes	Methods
Know the names of a range of snack foods from a café or fast-food place	Students can: ■ speak the words of a range of foods ■ write and spell correctly the words and associated phrases.	■ Flashcards ■ Drawings ■ Vocabulary lists ■ Tests on words and phrases ■ Listening to tape recordings ■ Making recordings
Know the names of fruit and vegetables	Students can: ■ speak the words and phrases for different fruits and vegetables ■ write and spell correctly the words and associated phrases.	■ Flashcards ■ Drawings ■ Vocabulary lists ■ Tests on words and phrases ■ Listening to tape recordings ■ Making recordings
Be able to hold a conversation where a student can buy a range of foods	Students can: ■ say the appropriate phrases both as a buyer and seller.	■ The above plus video recordings, use of artefacts etc.

TABLE 1.3   Topic analysis: planning document model

- Lesson by lesson objectives
- Lesson outcomes and assessment objectives
- Learning activities
- Teaching strategies
- Resources
- Homework tasks which enhance the learning in class
- Timing and pace.

with the learning outcomes in mind. The process is one in which the learning needs are identified, the assessment outcomes are specified and the teaching activities are planned to address these needs and outcomes. The focus for the teacher is not about what he or she is planning to teach but about what students are going to learn. By making this important paradigm shift, the teacher is empowered to plan with learning (rather than teaching) at the fore.

Further, by breaking down the topic even more and considering the learning outcomes in greater depth, the planning of the learning becomes, in our view, more proactive and more straightforward. It is possible to plan a unit lesson by lesson. Therefore, a planning document for such a unit of work can include the items listed in Table 1.3.

By moving towards this model for planning work, the prospects for differentiation become more realistic. Why? There are two reasons. The first is that the hard work of planning the outcomes of the lessons is done in advance. This enables all those involved in delivering the curriculum to see how it fits together – it brings coherence and cohesion. Second, it facilitates quality planning. It means that the teacher can think about the learning needs of each student in the class. The need for assessment is highlighted in this strategy – it emphasises that if a lesson is to be a valuable learning experience for the students then it needs to be pitched appropriately. By making assessment one of the priorities, this is then made a realistic possibility.

Planning work with students in mind

When planning a unit of work, it is helpful to picture the students who will be taught. This is where the issue of differentiation comes once more to the fore.

In schools with a setting policy, there is sometimes an assumption that the issue of differentiation has been addressed. In some ways this represents the shift that needs to occur. There has to be an acknowledgement that students have individual learning needs and that it is the role of the classroom teacher to act as a *learning agent*. However, by thinking of particular students in the class who represent the range of ability it is possible to start to produce a differentiated lesson within the parameters of five groups (i.e. the most able, able, middle ability, lower ability and least able within the parameters of the ability range).

TASK 3

Selecting a strategy for differentiation

The following task is designed to help you to consider the priority and strategies that might be employed to produce a differentiated programme.

Table 1.4 gives ten statements about differentiation. Decide whether each statement relates to input (what the teacher does), process (the work the students do) or outcome (the work that is assessed).

TABLE 1.4 Ten differentiation strategies

1 All the students in my classes work at their own level on different assignments, within a given topic.	**2** I divide my class into ability groups and each group does different work on the same topic.
3 I teach to the middle of my classes – all my students work on the same assignments.	**4** All the students complete common assignments but there is extension work for the most able.
5 Students select tasks for themselves.	**6** I structure the work so that the most able students progress quickly through the first parts of assignments and progress to the harder material.
7 I differentiate through output rather than input.	**8** Students work on common assignments but help one another.
9 Students work through the same exercises but at different rates – I differentiate through the work rate.	**10** All students attempt some aspects of the same topic but then have guided choices through a range of differentiated tasks.

Group the statements and produce a rank order of importance.

Justify your ranking.

The consequence of differentiating by input, process or outcome has implications for the middle manager thinking of developing a teaching programme (see Table 1.5).

TABLE 1.5 Input, process and outcome differentiation – benefits and consequences

Statement	Benefits of the approach	Consequences of the approach
Input	■ The students tackle work appropriately matched to their ability. ■ Possibility of assessment related to the input is enhanced. ■ A wide range of media can be utilised. ■ Resources can be planned around such matters as readability, ease of use by students.	■ At this stage the input needs to be carefully classified. ■ The teacher needs accurate baseline data on which to base the judgement. ■ Takes time to create high quality resources – 10 hours of teacher preparation time to produce one hour of student work.
Process	■ Students benefit from learning new skills and knowledge before they tackle assignments. ■ Study skills can be enhanced because they are introduced in a specific context. ■ A variety of tasks can be produced. ■ The process can be adapted readily to take account of progress. ■ Mechanisms can be built in to help students stay on task.	■ Students may not fulfil expectations if the process matching is inaccurate. ■ The variety of tasks can reduce teacher efficiency. ■ Careful monitoring is required to ensure that students make appropriate progress.

TABLE 1.5   *(cont'd)*

Statement	Benefits of the approach	Consequences of the approach
Outcome	■ Course objectives can be planned to be accessible to all. ■ The assessment depends entirely on the outcome. ■ No stigmatisation of students tackling different work. ■ Response reflects what student has achieved. ■ Students can exceed expectations.	■ Close monitoring is needed to ensure adequate challenge for the most able and realistic challenges for the least able.

Leading and managing projects

An essential part of an aspiring middle manager's development is the leading and management of projects. Certainly, in terms of a job application, it is essential that you have led a range of projects to conclusion successfully.

The features of a good project in this context are as follows.

■ There is a clearly defined need for the project – probably identified by pupil data or response.

■ The project leader has identified the overall strategy by the outcomes that will result from the successful implementation of the project.

■ The project leader has negotiated a plan with the management team (or the current team leader). This plan contains details such as budget, time plans and stage outcomes (i.e. at specified times during the project there will be outcomes which contribute to the whole effort).

This section is about leading a project and working with others.

Establishing a contract

If this process is to be effective and the benefits maximised there needs to be a clear contract. There are several stages to this.

1 *Negotiating the task.* The original idea may spring from a team meeting – the team leader presenting some ideas to the team – the development

plan or a chance meeting. Whatever the starting point, you need to consider what outcomes are required and how feasible the aims of the project are. It may be that you are very keen to pursue a particular topic but that the team leader does not agree. This needs to be tackled sensitively and you need to consider the reasons for the project carefully and seek to persuade the team leader or manager.

One way is to discuss with the team leader exactly what is necessary to complete the task. One outcome of such a discussion might be that you accept that the job is beyond your skill – at this time. However, if the team leader is able to support you and give strong and positive direction, then much can be achieved.

2 *Deciding what to do*. For any job to be done there are stages. These include, as a minimum:

- *Planning* – this is where the job is broken down into its essential parts. An audit of what is current practice may be necessary. One outcome should be a statement of intent and purpose. This should include a timescale.

- *Process* – this is where the job is actually done. This may include negotiating with individuals, creating resources, presenting information, reporting findings etc. The main outcome is that the task is completed.

- *Evaluation* – no process is complete without some evaluation of what has been done. This may simply be a reflection of what went well and what was less successful. For a developmental task, the evaluation should also include a consideration of how the teacher has planned and carried out the task. Where the work has involved leading and managing others, time should be allowed for you to reflect on your interpersonal skills.

- *Review* – this is an essential part of the cycle. It needs to include a conclusion on the task and a recommendation on how the work could be developed in the future. At the basic level, it is about how the job should be carried out next time.

3 *Timing and reporting on progress*. An important part of the process is to agree a timescale. The timing should complement the plan and there should be identifiable outcomes. This negotiation is an important means of providing support for the teacher. Also, it will enable the work of the team to be kept to time.

4 *Supporting the teacher*. The process outlined above is the means by which the teacher is supported. The team leader and the team members agree the outcomes and the timing. Thus, the team leader is in a position to

offer the appropriate amount of support. Experienced staff, operating within their 'comfort zone' may need little guidance – they can be directed and then can 'get on with it'. Others need more guidance.

5 *Learning from the job.* The process of working together has to be a developmental one and allocating time for reflection is important to the future work of the team. It is also worthwhile for you to reflect on the teachers' response to your direction. Has the amount of direction and guidance been appropriate? Further, how might you continue the developmental process with the team as a whole and the teachers as individuals?

_____ Delegation _____

The practice of delegation is fundamental. Team leaders have a responsibility, not only to the team but also to themselves to delegate effectively. If a team is to act as a unit, then opportunities for them to collaborate are essential. The processes outlined in this chapter provide the teacher with a framework that not only encourages teamwork but also makes it inescapable. This is a feature that is worthy of reflection.

At the start of this section, we referred to the need to develop people, not only to maximise the effectiveness of the team but also as a wider responsibility to the profession as a whole. Many teachers move schools in order to gain promotion. Teachers as individuals and schools as organisations benefit from the cross-fertilisation of ideas that this system inevitably brings. However, much is lost when an experienced teacher finds it necessary to leave a school to obtain the promotion desired. It is desirable that there should be an element of succession planning within the system. The team leader can use a vision for the team to develop a successor. Therefore, to maximise these possibilities, the team leader should see the team in the context of succession, recognising there will be those who do not want the promotion, the threshold assessment and all that goes with it.

As well as the teaching responsibilities of their professionals, schools and colleges still need to have management tasks carried out. Tasks include setting and monitoring budgets, resourcing teaching and learning, providing a well-qualified and competent staff, liaising with students, parents, employers and the wider community, and responding to government requirements. Responsibility for these tasks can be concentrated in the hands of a small number of people or widely dispersed among the staff.

However senior or junior their formal position in the organisation may be, managers are both agents of change and bulwarks against it. In a stable environment their role is one of continuing review and improvement. In turbulent times they may have to filter the pressures created by demands for change, so that those who work in their area of responsibility can carry on in as secure an environment as possible. Good management involves supporting colleagues, assisting them with resources and providing staff development opportunities to cope with the changes that are required. And, uncomfortable though it may sometimes be, their own work and that of others requires monitoring and evaluating so that standards are maintained and, where possible, improved.

All this requires managers to have an understanding of how organisations work, how people are motivated and how change can be brought about successfully. It requires an awareness of the tasks of leadership. And it requires the ability to investigate problems and issues within their area of responsibility and, if necessary, more widely in order to generate new ideas and approaches which can keep the organisation operating well and delivering what is required.

Starting to look for a post

As time progresses and you acquire experience, you will start to look for a post. It is important that you are aware of the skills and attributes that are required for this new job at the planning stage.

TASK 4

Analysing a job description

When posts are advertised it is customary to provide candidates with a job description. Below is such a description for the Head of Subject in a large comprehensive school. This task is designed to enable you to identify the skills and experiences needed for the post.

Read the job description for the Head of Subject. Using this document identify:

■ the core purpose and its implications

■ the key attributes that are being sought by the school

■ how a teacher can plan to meet these attributes.

Job description for a Head of Subject

Accountable to: Deputy Head (Quality of Teaching) and ultimately the Headteacher.

The Head of Subject is responsible for all aspects of the subject in the school.

Core purpose of the Head of Subject

The core purpose of a head of subject is to provide professional leadership and management to secure high quality teaching, effective use of resources and improved standards of learning and achievement for all pupils in the care of the department.

The specific tasks associated with the role of head of subject

1 Leading, managing and developing a subject or curriculum area.

The tasks associated with the role of head of subject are specifically to:

- lead the development and implementation of policies and practices in line with school policies
- advise the Headteacher and Deputy Headteacher of developments in the subject
- develop and ensure the effective delivery of ICT as part of the subject portfolio
- prepare development plans as necessary
- promote the subject in school and beyond
- produce reports for the Headteacher and Deputy Headteacher, as required.

The outcomes associated with this element are to lead a subject so that *teachers* will:

- be consistent in their practice
- be consistent in their implementation of policies
- use the outcomes of department self-evaluation to develop practices that result in pupil progress
- collaborate to implement development plans.

The outcomes associated with this element are to lead a subject so that *pupils* will:

- actively participate in learning
- produce work and assignments in response to curriculum demands (including homework)
- conform to the school's behaviour policy.

The outcomes associated with this element are to work as part of a *team of heads of subject* who:

- are consistent in their practice
- share good practice with other subject leaders

- act as role models in teaching pupils effectively
- act as role models in managing pupils effectively
- act as role models in demonstrating professional curriculum leadership.

2 **Impacting on the educational progress of pupils beyond those assigned to the teacher.**

The outcomes associated with this element are to lead the subject so that *pupils* will:

- achieve high standards in public examinations
- progress to the next stage of their education with confidence and enthusiasm
- show sustained improvement in the subject
- understand how to improve their studies
- know their academic targets
- be enthusiastic about the subject
- contribute to the maintenance of a purposeful working environment.

3 **Leading, developing and enhancing the teaching practice of others and managing staff.**

The tasks associated with this element are specifically to:

- Implement school policy on monitoring and evaluating the work of the department. This will include undertaking lesson observation, giving feedback to staff and, where appropriate, setting targets to improve the quality of teaching.
- Lead the production and updating of schemes of work. These should ensure curriculum coverage, continuity and progression in the subject for all pupils, including those of high ability and those with special needs.
- Coordinate the production of tests and examinations of the appropriate standard across the subject area.
- Keep parents well informed about their child's achievement in the subject and ensure that all information sent to parents is of a high standard.
- Direct and supervise the work of teachers delivering the subject.
- Lead the production of the subject handbook and update it regularly.
- Provide information and participate in threshold assessment and performance management processes.

The outcomes associated with this element are that *teachers* of the subject will:

- work together as a team with shared aims

- plan and deliver lessons, using the subject programme of study, where objectives are shared and reviewed
- support the aims of the school and understand how their team role relates to the school's aims
- have detailed job descriptions which set out their responsibilities and duties
- ensure that all pupils are prepared adequately for public examinations
- keep parents well informed about their child's achievement in the subject and ensure that all information sent to parents is of a high standard
- monitor the academic progress of the pupils in their teaching groups
- advise the Head of Subject on matters affecting the pupils in their groups.

4 **Monitoring and accountability.**

The tasks associated with this element are to:

- provide information, advice and analysis for the Headteacher and other senior managers so that they can understand the issues affecting the progress of individuals or groups in the subject
- monitor, evaluate and review the impact of interventions and resources for the subject
- respond to other adults and agencies who require up-to-date information about the subject presented in a concise and accurate manner.

5 **Any other duties as required.**

The core purpose is stated at the start of the document. There are a number of key attributes stated in this job description and these are:

- leading and developing – this relates to the production of policies and also to the work of the team
- responsibility
- managing, directing and supervising
- coordinating and implementing.

These skills and attributes are essential for the middle manager. They can be acquired through a range of projects and initiatives.

The most important characteristic of the aspiring middle manager is to be an excellent teacher. By focusing attention on this aspect of their work and developing projects around this core function, the teacher will be in a strong position to take on responsibility in whatever form it is offered.

_____ Summary _____

At some point in your career you need to think through what you want to do in the long term. Whether you are keen to progress to middle management or simply prepare for threshold assessment the key features are:

- set the goal of becoming an excellent teacher
- learn the qualities which OfSTED seek when making judgements
- incorporate these features into classroom practice
- focus on getting the teaching and learning right before looking beyond the classroom
- choose projects which directly impact on pupil achievement
- establish a clear remit for the project and agree a contract
- take the opportunity to work alongside others on projects and invite them to join yours
- seek out feedback and use it to develop your expertise
- look at the next job – see what skills and attributes are required and plan for them
- think years ahead – teachers who invest in their schools and in themselves will always grow as professionals.

_____ References _____

Applebee, A. (1989) 'The Enterprise We Are Part of: Learning to Teach', *Developments in Learning and Assessment*, Eds. Murphy, P. and Moon, B., (1990) London: Hodder and Stoughton.

Bennett, N. (1987) 'Processes in the Post-Plowden Era', *Developments in Learning and Assessment,* Eds. Murphy, P. and Moon, B., (1990) London: Hodder and Stoughton.

Bowring-Carr, C. and West-Burnham, J. (1997) *Effective Learning in Schools*, London: Pearson.

Cohen, L. and Manion, L. (1977) *A Guide to Teaching Practice,* London: Methuen.

Combs, A. (1965) 'The Professional Education of Teachers', *A Guide to Teaching Practice*, Cohen, L. and Manion, L. (1977), London: Methuen.

Hargreaves, A. (1994) *Changing Teachers, Changing Times*, London: Continuum.

MacGilchrist, B., Myers, K. and Reed, J. (1997) *The Intelligent School*, London: Paul Chapman Publishing Ltd.

OfSTED (2003) *Handbook for Inspecting Secondary Schools*, London: OfSTED.

Percival, A. and Tranter, S. (2004) *How to Run your School Successfully*, London: Continuum.

Skilbeck, M. (1989) 'A Changing Social and Educational Context', *Policies for the Curriculum,* Eds. Moon, B., Murphy, P. and Raynor, J., Open University, London: Hodder and Stoughton.

Steps on the ladder

– making the application and preparing for interview

Introduction

The thought of having some responsibility, taking the first or another step on the career ladder can be very exciting. It should be! Working with others but having the opportunity to shape the way things are done is a tremendous privilege, but it needs preparation and careful thought.

Preparing to lead and manage is not something to be entered into lightly – middle managers are increasingly responsible for the curriculum, pupil progress, personnel management, health and safety, and budgets – to name but a few. You do not need to have experience in all of these areas but an understanding of them is essential. People will depend on you for advice and guidance – the selection process will help the school to find out whether you are the right person to do the job, but it's equally important to see whether it's what you want as well.

In this chapter we are going to consider building up a personal portfolio, preparing your CV, writing letters of application, preparing for interview and some typical questions. Many selection processes place less reliance on the interview as the sole component of the process. It is not uncommon to be asked to teach a sample lesson, write a paper or lead a meeting for highly contested posts – we discuss how to prepare for these. But first we explore what it means to be a leader and manager in a school – and why you might want to do it.

Being a modern subject leader

What does this mean for the middle manager? For the aspiring subject leader it means the following.

- The curriculum is delivered equitably – there should be schemes of work which map out the entire curriculum coverage for the subject.
- The team is led in a professional manner. This means that there are policies which address such matters as assessment, equal opportunities, behaviour etc. Further, these are policies in practice – they are part of the daily life in the team and are monitored effectively. Of course, the team may include teachers and other staff (for example teaching assistants (TAs), higher-level teaching assistants (HLTAs), support staff, ancillary staff) and their professional needs will have to be integrated into the team plans and policies.
- The subject leader has a vision for the subject – the middle manager is secure in respect of the place of the subject in the curriculum and knows how to realise the vision.

- The team is constantly evaluating its own performance (in a way that matches school self-evaluation processes) with a view to continuous improvement.
- There are sufficient quality controls such that the quality of the teams' work is assured.

Professionalism

The word 'professional' has been subjected to considerable misuse over recent years. For many, a professional is someone who does a job and gets paid for it. We hear of the professional footballer and the professional rugby player to name but two. However, some attributes of the more traditional professions give us insight into the principle of the 'professional teacher' (see Table 2.1).

TABLE 2.1 Attributes of some of the professions

Profession	Attribute	Implications for the teacher
Medicine	■ Expectation that the professional will continue to develop professionally.	■ Teachers continue their professional development by undertaking Master degree courses etc. There is an expectation that this is the case – the portability of courses means that credits from one course can be put together with others.
	■ Pre-registration period before a doctor is fully qualified to practise.	■ The induction year for teachers has been given additional rigour in that if a teacher fails the induction year they cannot work as a teacher again.
	■ Professional body which represents and regulates the profession.	■ The teachers' associations are, in the main, trade unions, which have a representative but not a regulatory function.
		■ The General Teaching Council is a regulatory body but is not necessarily a representational one.

TABLE 2.1 *(cont'd)*

Profession	Attribute	Implications for the teacher
Law	■ Candidates for the profession take articles or pupillage – there is an expectation that professional competence will be acquired over a period of time.	■ There is a stated belief that the art of advocacy has to be acquired and learned from the more experienced.
	■ Pupils assist barristers in preparing for cases.	■ The practice of the law is one where the lawyer's skill is rehearsed and guided.
	■ Service and expertise is recognised by the award of Queen's Counsel status.	■ Experience is valued and recognised.
Clergy	■ A young cleric will act as a curate under the direction of an experienced priest.	■ Recognition that the clergy is vocational. It is a commitment to the faith and to the role of the clergy in society.

Although the attributes have been carefully selected – and it would be naive to believe that it is as straightforward as these attributes suggest – there are important implications for teachers.

We shall now consider the features of being a professional in the educational context. There are a number of elements which should be included.

What it means to be a professional teacher

First, the commitment to updating and developing subject knowledge. In the main, the subject knowledge acquired as part of a first degree is beyond that expected of a teacher. However, there are still a significant number of teachers who have inadequate ICT skills; also, there is often a need for staff to be redeployed and new skills to be acquired. The culture needs to be one in which teachers expect to develop their subject knowledge. Further, there is a need for teachers to develop their leadership and management skills. While there is no substitute for experience, any reflection is enhanced when underpinned by theory. This is the value of Masters degrees which specialise in management in education. More will be said of this elsewhere in the book.

Second, there is recognition among teachers that skills take time to acquire. A useful metaphor for a teacher's career is that of a marathon rather than a sprint. The rhythm of the academic year means that certain issues emerge only once a year. For example, when preparing students for public examinations teachers employ a range of strategies to help their students to retain and apply the knowledge they have acquired. Particular difficulties can arise with any strategy – a reflective teacher may consider the solution but will not be able to test it out until it recurs, perhaps the following year. There may be procedural issues which do not emerge until the system is tried out – for example, options systems at Key Stage 4, arrangements for Key Stage tests etc. Again, these events occur annually. For some professionals, issues may arise once in a professional lifetime and the opportunity for reflection may not benefit the process directly. A year head may have to deal with the death of a child. For most teachers this is a very rare occurrence. It will require sound skills and will test the school as an organisation and the teacher as a professional. The middle manager may never need to call on these skills again. However, such an incident illustrates the need for professional dialogue between teachers in posts of responsibility. No one can be expected to have experienced every situation and have the perfect solution. There needs to be, in us all, recognition that skills and experiences are acquired and that there is a wealth of experience in every school. The older teachers are those with the most experience – this needs to be both acknowledged and valued.

The definition of a professional is, in some ways, specific to the phase of education. For example, the intellectual demands made of a teacher working in a school where the vast majority go on to university, many to Oxbridge, differ from those needed by someone teaching in an education action zone. This is not to say that children attending these schools do not have the same or similar intellectual needs, but the comparative demands are an issue.

Your personal portfolio

Newly qualified teachers join the profession with a set of induction targets. Having progressed through the training phase, these teachers will have agreed with their tutors what areas for development are appropriate focuses for the first year. During this year you will have reviews and these should be referenced to your induction targets. It is good practice to set up a file in which these documents, which form a record of your professional development, can be kept. A lever arch file works well – you can section it using dividers and keep it up to date. Some other sections might include:

- *Qualifications* – in this section keep a copy of your GCSE, A level, degree, PGCE and other qualifications. The originals need to be kept in a safe place as you will need to produce them when you apply for other jobs.

- *Induction record* – in this section keep your PGCE reports and induction records so that you have the path that takes you from your training to your first year.

- *INSET record* – you will often be asked to list the courses you have attended and keeping a copy of the flyer, certificates of attendance and any other relevant materials will help you to compile this list.

- *Performance reviews* – in this section keep a copy of professional reviews. You should have a review each year and this should include a lesson observation. Being able to demonstrate how you have progressed and developed is very important.

- *Exam results record* – having a track record of successful teaching that leads to students getting very good or excellent results is increasingly important. Being able to show how you have done this over your career will put you in a favourable light.

- *Letters, memos and congratulatory notes* – parents will write to thank you, students will do so as well. Hopefully, senior staff will commend your work – this may be in the form of the school newsletter or a personally written note. Keeping these records your success (and is also a great tonic if you have a series of bad days!). If your work is mentioned in an OfSTED report or local authority review then add this too.

- *Records of projects and examples of documents or other artefacts* – as you are involved in projects, working groups and development activities then keep records of what you are doing so that you can refer to them. Keeping an example of a booklet, a lesson plan or resource that you produced is good practice as you can show it to others and possibly use it in another context.

- *Your Criminal Records Bureau clearance.*

Keeping this personal portfolio is a useful way of charting your progress, but also prepares all of the material and evidence you will need for threshold assessment.

Before you start on the business of job applications, it is beneficial to discuss your ideas with a senior colleague. Having a focused discussion on your strengths and weaknesses, using the opportunity to audit your skills will enable you to assess your own progress before you start to think further about your applications.

Motivation

Having considered what it is to be a professional in the world of education as a whole and in a particular sphere, the next task is to consider why a teacher wants to be a middle manager. The motivation for the role is important and will certainly be a major factor in determining the success of both an application and the postholder in themselves.

TASK 5

Identifying your motivation

What motivates people is an important dimension of leadership and management. Being able to understand what motivates your colleagues can help you to challenge their work, and also enable you to 'tap' into their skills to mutual benefit. Also, if things go wrong, being able to demonstrate an understanding of their motives can go a long way to securing a solution to the difficulty. Before you try to develop understanding of others, however, you first need to look at yourself.

For this task we ask you to consider some of the reasons why people seek promotion. List the reasons and use your list to consider:

- In what sense do they apply to you?
- Do you consider these desirable motives?
- How can you show that you possess these motives?

For some teachers economic necessity is a strong motivation for seeking promotion. Rarely, however, is it the sole reason for applying for a promoted post. The reason is not just that the financial reward is not that great, but that which motivates most teachers is the desire to do their best for the pupils in their charge. However, while the individual teacher may be able to exert influence over those in their charge, the motivation for seeking promotion is a desire to extend this sphere of influence over a wider group.

The issue of power is a significant one. The power a middle manager is able to wield over a group varies considerably – it depends a good deal on the hierarchical structure of the school. However, middle managers are increasingly required to be responsible and accountable for the outcomes of their department or team and so there is a considerable challenge to be considered here. Power is complex; if we consider for a moment the way in which many subject teams operate. There will be a head of department who will be the line manager for the teachers who teach the subject – however, it is not unusual for some members of that teaching group to have other responsibilities. (In my case, as head of mathematics the head-teacher, deputy head, an assistant head and a head of year all taught the subject). In what sense, therefore, was I the line manager when there were people who reported to others (and carried out their performance reviews and so on) and, indeed, one member of the team was the person ultimately responsible for the school? The hierarchical construct that can be found in business and commerce, for example, is not entirely applicable to the school context. Add to this the fact that for most of the working day a teacher works alone (if one can be alone with 30 children!). The notion of power in a school is complex and relies far more on influence. However, there are significant matters where the head of department exerts considerable power – the deployment of teachers to classes, purchasing, budget control, class composition and so on. Wanting to be a head of department for power alone is fraught with danger. Power in a school isn't always as apparent or clear-cut as it may first appear.

Other motives include the desire to have responsibility – to be the one who leads, organises and makes things happen. In some cases this can be because you have tried and succeeded in making changes or organising things, conversely because you think you can do better than the person who you see doing the job. If the next step is part of a career plan, then thinking about how the next move will help you achieve your goals is an important step in preparing for the next role. In Table 2.2 we raise a number of issues relating to the responsibilities that different middle management posts carry and the implications for the postholder.

TABLE 2.2 Middle management posts: responsibilities and implications

Post	Examples of responsibilities	Implications for the postholder
Head of Department	■ Will have line responsibility for staff and decide their deployment.	■ Needs to consider the nature of management.
	■ Will be involved in recruitment of staff.	■ Needs to clarify his/her staffing policies and plan accordingly.

TABLE 2.2   (*cont'd*)

Post	Examples of responsibilities	Implications for the postholder
	■ Will have budget responsibility.	■ Will need to develop systems for monitoring expenditure and accounting for monies spent.
	■ Will appraise staff.	■ Appraisal is becoming more closely linked to pay and the postholder will need to consider his/her processes with care.
	■ Will be seen as a senior member of staff.	■ This may require you to change your habits – you may have to distance yourself from particular situations to preserve your impartiality. If taking on a new role might bring you into conflict with a friend, you will need to consider how you are going to deal with this.
	■ As a group, heads of departments will be responsible for majority of the curriculum.	■ As a head of department, there will be opportunities for collaboration – but there has been a tendency in some organisations for heads of departments to compete against one another.
Subject coordinator in a primary school	■ Will have responsibility for the development of the subject.	■ There may not be parity in the treatment of subject areas.
	■ For a core subject or national initiative (such as Literacy and Numeracy) the role will have a high profile.	■ The role relies on coordinating skills.

TABLE 2.2   *(cont'd)*

Post	Examples of responsibilities	Implications for the postholder
Year leader	■ Will recommend the disciplinary sanctions applied to pupils.	■ Authority is over pupils rather than staff.
	■ Will make decisions about pupils.	■ There may be difficulties in the interface between the pastoral and academic traditions.
	■ Will have to conduct investigations into incidents.	■ Some situations will involve people expressing strong emotions – you will encounter situations where the adult's behaviour has been a significant factor in the incident.
Cross-curricular coordinator	■ Nature of cross-curricular initiatives will often receive significant senior management support.	■ The cross-curricular coordinator will need strong organisational skills and the ability to enthuse.
Head of Section (in FE)	■ May have to draw up contracts with teachers.	■ May spend a significant amount of time involved in contractual negotiations. In some cases the postholder will have little influence over the contracts and this may weaken his/her status in the organisation.
	■ Will have line management responsibility.	■ Issues of communication are brought to the fore when managing part-time staff.
	■ May be the only contact with the hierarchical structures (particularly the part-time lecturers, paid on an hourly basis).	■ In some FE establishments some lecture programmes are delivered in the evenings – this may affect the control the postholder is able to exert.

However, if we take a more enlightened view of power it is the power to change things for the better. It is about managing a team to bring about change and to improve the quality of education. This is a personal motivation.

Frustration

In some cases the motivation for seeking a middle management role may be frustration. This frustration may arise from observing problematic features of the educational experience. These features can include:

- *Philosophical issues* – perhaps it is school policy to teach in sets and the teacher believes in the benefits of mixed ability teaching. The school (or team) may have chosen a particular course and the teacher does not fully support the programme.
- *Pedagogical issues* – the teaching culture of the school or team may be at variance with the teacher's views.
- *Desire to progress in the profession* – the teacher may simply want to be the one who leads the team!

Anyone whose motivation is based on frustration needs to be careful. While it is surely a factor which influences all those who have progressed, there has to be a desire to exert influence and a certain level of disquiet. However, the prospective middle manager needs to be wary of exchanging one set of frustrations for another. Also, if the frustration is in any sense negative, this can be detrimental to the recruiting process.

Opportunity

For some middle managers, promotion comes from opportunity. A year head may leave unexpectedly, there may be a national initiative, the head of department may offer opportunities to a teacher – these are examples where the teacher has the chance to prove worthy of the post. The opportunity to be the 'Acting . . .' is one which offers considerable scope for advancement. Many of us have sought promotion because of the encouragement we have been given from our colleagues. This may come from one's head of department, a deputy headteacher or headteacher. Indeed, it is an enlightened manager who takes the task of staff development with sufficient seriousness to recommend that a teacher seeks promotion. However, it is part of the profession's responsibility to itself to develop the skills and attributes in order to facilitate this progression.

For many teachers, however, there is a strong desire to improve the lot of pupils and to increase the opportunities available to them. In some cases we may have witnessed inequality or unfairness. For some of us, there is a recognition that we owe the quality of our lives to the educational opportunities we have been offered. There has to be an element of this in all teachers if they are to succeed and if they are to unlock the potential that exists in the pupils they teach.

However, the mission of the teacher and, in this context, the middle manager should not be abused. It needs to be acknowledged and valued by school leaders and government. Often, teachers work tirelessly to improve and create opportunities and their service goes unrecognised. Many teachers will, and do, work hard and the remuneration offered does not match either the effort or the result. The altruism of teachers cannot be overstated and its recognition is a challenge for all those in management roles in schools. Middle managers should not only recognise this in themselves but also acknowledge it in others. You will need to consider this carefully when preparing to make an application and further still when taking on a middle management post.

Information sources

The main source of information about job vacancies is, of course, *The Times Educational Supplement*. The jobs section is classified and categorised according to phase of school and subject order.

The quality of advertisements does vary but most contain the following information.

- Name and address of the school.
- The title of the post and the allowance paid. If this is not specified, either by category or in the advert, it needs to be clarified.
- Brief details about the school, the post and how to apply.

In many cases the school's fax number and, increasingly, e-mail and website details are included. There are cases where the entire process is conducted electronically – details about the school, the application process and the necessary forms and documents are available only from the website and have to be returned by e-mail.

Whatever the process, it is useful to visit the school website because it gives a valuable insight into how the school operates. Certainly, it will count against you if you do not as it is such an easy media to use. The way in which the website is organised can be an indicator of the school's attitude towards ICT (information and communications technology). Some of the better school websites include the following:

- the most recent OfSTED report
- recent examination results
- a homepage for parents
- the headteacher's e-mail address
- an area written by students
- the school prospectus
- virtual tours of the school
- newsletters
- events and happenings.

Most advertisements will invite candidates to request further details which outline the application procedure. An application pack will comprise some of the following elements:

- about the school – this may include the school prospectus
- about the job – this may include a person specification and a job specification
- details about the department (if it is a subject post)
- details about the pastoral system
- an application form
- details such as the closing date, interview dates etc.

_____ Planning an application _____

In this section we are going to consider the following.

1 How to analyse the information available to you.

2 How to read the person specification.

3 How to read the job specification.

4 Writing a letter of application and completing an application form.

5 Writing a CV.

6 Sending the covering letter and application form.

7 Interview preparation and etiquette.

8 Questions to consider.

9 Accepting the post.

1 How to analyse the information available to you

Any candidate for a teaching post in a school will need to know basic information about the school and ask some questions about the job they are considering.

TASK 6

Analysing information about a school

Consider the facts about the school and analyse the information.

1 Think about what the implications would be for you in your current role and school.

2 Think about how you will demonstrate your preparation for this post with your background.

The first thing to consider is the size of the school. If you are currently teaching in a small school and the new post is in a much larger one, you will need to think about how to show that you are aware of the challenges you will face. The team with which you will work may be larger or smaller, and there will be interpersonal skills to consider. Similarly, if the school is on a split site then an awareness of the implications of this is imperative. Some split-site schools operate on an upper school/lower school model, others split the year groups vertically (with half of the year group at each site). While the former can lead to teachers moving from one site to another, the latter can be organised so that half the teachers of, say, English work on one site and, the other half on the second site. Investigating how the school is organised is important because it gives you an idea about whether this is what you want, and also about how you can (and if you can) make it work.

There are a whole range of other factors that are worthy of consideration. When you look at the website or prospectus, do the children look happy? Does the way in which the school is presented attract you to the school? Making a decision about where you work is a serious one – try to distance yourself from the lure of extra money and promotion because getting it wrong can have disastrous consequences personally and professionally.

It is important to have a look at the OfSTED report(s) and the school statistics. If the school is very successful and the department isn't then it is likely they will be looking for someone who can demonstrate an awareness of improvement and can show the skills necessary to bring about that improvement. A school that is in some difficulty will look for teachers who will be part of school improvement teams. A common factor is that most schools look to improve. The degree of challenge and the imperative for action may vary, but the commonality of the school improvement agenda is consistent. Think about how the things you have done, the projects you have involved yourself in – and indeed your own teaching – have contributed to your department or team's improvement cycle.

The main question to ask at this stage is whether the profile of the new school makes you want to work there. Does this seem a place that you could work in? If it is important to you to work as part of a close team, where you know each other well, then a large team of 12 may not be the one for you.

However, you need to take care when analysing these documents – there may be issues which have not been tackled in the material. Some schools take their publicity very seriously and there are some indicators to consider.

- *A wealth of information* – that is well presented indicates a school that takes its marketing seriously. It wants to present itself in a favourable light. Of course, by giving you a lot of information, you will be expected to have read it and be able to comment on it.

- *Paucity of information* – some very successful schools do not consider it important to promote themselves. Such a school may have the view that teachers will want to work there because it is what it is. Alternatively, it might be that there is no one who can collate the material. This may be the case in a small school or one where there has been a reduction in teaching staff. The question to ask of yourself is whether the lack of a prospectus is a major issue for you. Do you consider publicity important? Could you improve it if you joined that school?

- *Information is inaccurate or incomplete* – the school may be in difficulties and so may choose to give very brief details. The challenge of a failing or struggling school is considerable and the candidate needs to consider how, as a middle manager, they will address it. Alternatively, things may have changed over a very short period of time and there has been no opportunity to review promotional materials. It is worthwhile being charitable, otherwise an opportunity may be lost.

- *Details about the post are vague* – the allowance to be paid may not be stated. This is a real warning sign because the post may change significantly – there may be budget constraints that are unresolved. The details of remuneration should be clear. It is important to clarify such details before you make an application.

2   How to read the person specification

There is a growing practice in appointment procedures to include a person specification. Such specifications are commonly in two sections – essential attributes and desirable attributes.

The 'essential' part of the specification means that without all the attributes listed you will not be considered for the post. However, for posts which are difficult to fill, schools may be prepared to waive some of these criteria. The person specification must be read carefully. You must ensure that you demonstrate all the essential elements and as many of the desirable criteria as possible.

The criteria will be assessed by some or all of:

- letter of application
- reference
- curriculum vitae
- interview process.

TASK 7

Responding to a person specification

Read the person specification in Table 2.3 and decide how a selection panel will assess whether the candidate meets the criteria – e.g. by CV, interview, references or letter of application.

TABLE 2.3   Person specification for head of modern languages (MFL)

Criteria	Essential	Desirable	Assessed by
Qualifications	■ First degree in MFL.	■ Higher degree in MFL.	
	■ Speaks more than one language.	■ Qualified to at least A level in a second language.	
Experience	■ Taught first language for at least ten years.	■ Taught more than one language.	

TABLE 2.3 (cont'd)

Criteria	Essential	Desirable	Assessed by
	■ Evidence of successful teaching to A level.	■ Taught in more than one school.	
	■ Evidence of successful project management.	■ Taught second language to at least GCSE level.	
	■ Evidence of wider curriculum involvement.	■ Experienced at managing change.	
Personal attributes	■ Commitment.		
	■ Integrity.		
	■ Adaptability to changing circumstances and new ideas.		
	■ Sense of humour.		
Skills and competencies	■ ICT capability.	■ Evidence of interest in curriculum development.	
	■ Can plan, prioritise and organise.		
	■ Can demonstrate high-level organisational skills.	■ A commitment to promoting high-quality teaching and evidence of having raised standards.	
	■ Excellent classroom practitioner.		
	■ Clear written and spoken communication.		

3   How to read the job specification

The job specification is about the broader details of the job. It specifies the tasks for which the responsibility is given. It will include a range of managerial and leadership functions.

TASK 8 ————————————————————————————————

Responding to a job description

Many schools use the *National Standards for Subject Leaders* to devise their job descriptions and this task challenges you to consider how you would respond to this job description (see Table 2.4).

TABLE 2.4   A middle manager's job description

Job description for a middle manager	Your response
Strategic direction and development	
■ To develop and implement policies and practices for the subject which reflect the school's commitment to high achievement, effective teaching and learning.	
■ To create a climate which enables other staff to develop and maintain positive attitudes towards the subject and also confidence in teaching it.	
■ Use data effectively to identify pupils who are underachieving in the subject and, where necessary, create and implement effective plans of actions to support those pupils.	
Teaching and learning	
■ Ensure curriculum coverage, continuity and progression in the subject for all pupils.	
■ Ensure that teachers are clear about the teaching objectives in lessons, understand the sequence of teaching and learning in the subject, and communicate such information to pupils.	
■ Provide guidance on the choice of appropriate teaching and learning methods.	
■ Establish and implement clear policies and practices for assessing, recording and reporting on pupil achievement.	

TABLE 2.4   *(cont'd)*

Job description for a middle manager	Your response

Leading and managing staff

- Help staff to achieve constructive working relationships with pupils.

- Establish clear expectations and constructive working relationships among staff involved with the subject, including through team working and mutual support. Devolve responsibilities and delegate tasks.

- Sustain your own motivation, and where possible, that of other staff.

- Appraise staff as required.

- Ensure that the headteacher, senior managers and governors are well informed about subject policies, plans and priorities, the success in meeting objectives and targets and subject-related professional development plans.

Efficient and effective deployment of staff and resources

- Establish staffing and resource needs for the subject and advise the headteacher and senior managers of likely priorities.

- Deploy staff, or advise the headteacher on the deployment of staff.

- Ensure the effective and efficient management and organisation of learning resources.

- Ensure that there is a safe working and learning environment in which risks are properly assessed.

The objective of this exercise is not that the middle manager should demonstrate an ability to do all of the tasks but that the middle manager can demonstrate the competencies required. One way in which the applicant can do this, both in the letter of application and in the interview process, is to describe an initiative which has demonstrated expertise in these areas and which shows possession of ideas on how these areas might be tackled.

The recruitment process for a middle manager is crucial to the success of a school. A headteacher has to assess – using the application, the references and the interview data – whether the candidate has the ability to do the job or not. Not only is a teacher being recruited, but also a manager.

4 Writing a letter of application and completing an application form

Writing a letter of application for a job is more difficult than completing an application form because there is no fixed structure to the task.

The main points about application forms are obvious, but it is surprising how many worthy candidates prejudice their applications by a failure to act on them. Table 2.5 gives guidance on this.

TABLE 2.5 Points to remember when completing an application form

---

- Answer all the questions. If a question is not applicable, write N/A next to it.
- Write or type in black – your application will be photocopied for the interview process.
- List your qualifications in chronological order.
- Emphasise any qualifications specified in the person description.
- Use any space which asks for details of recent training to illustrate your preparation for the job.
- Include your degree class and A level grades. GCSE and 'O' levels are less relevant but may be required.
- There is normally a space asking about hobbies and interests – include details which demonstrate your personal qualities.
- Absence record – this is becoming increasingly common and it is important to quote this accurately as it will normally be included as part of a reference.
- Criminal record – be honest, even about speeding fines, as an application may not proceed without accurate police checks.
- Referees – include the name, title, postal address, e-mail address, telephone and fax numbers.
- Use the space for the letter of application on the form as indicated. Set out the letter as if you were writing a formal letter.
- Make sure that you follow the application procedure exactly and that you include all the details requested.

Writing a letter is in some ways more difficult, but it does give you the opportunity to explain why you should be considered. Having used the information to analyse the school, it is important that your letter shows that you have considered the strengths and weaknesses of the school and the post for which you are applying. Your letter should cover the following points:

- relevant experience
- successful management of change
- management training undertaken
- achievements in teaching and learning – it is worthwhile including your previous student exam results where appropriate
- extracurricular involvement.

One way to construct such a letter is to 'brainstorm' all the points to be included in the letter. The letter could follow the template shown in Table 2.6.

TABLE 2.6 Application letter model

- What you do currently and what job you are applying to do.
- What your current role is and how this has prepared you for the job,
- Why you want to do the job at this school.
- Your philosophy of teaching the subject (or teaching in general).
- Your interest in the subject.
- Your involvement in the wider life of the school.

Sometimes you may be asked to describe, for example, a change you managed or a problem you resolved – the application must fulfil all that is requested.

The letter should be no more than two sides of A4 in a readable font. It should be enthusiastic in tone and should be unique, individual and convey the person who is applying for the job.

A successful letter is one that gives the impression of being personal and that expresses your personality. When you write a letter ask yourself the following questions.

Do you:

- set out the key elements of the position being applied for and the reason why you want to do the job
- explain how your experience has prepared you for this job
- explain how you will be able to do the functional aspects of the job
- identify your strengths as a classroom practitioner
- describe briefly a project you have led, the impact it had on pupil achievement and the lessons learnt
- explain how you will lead and manage the team to incorporate new ideas
- show that you have researched the school and have thought about what you have to offer
- convey an enthusiasm not only for the job but also for school life in general
- write with conviction
- write clearly, accurately, concisely – with no spelling or punctuation mistakes?

It is very tempting, when applying for jobs during a busy working week, to try to 'cut and paste' from one letter to another. Try to resist the temptation because it is very easy to make errors of the kind where the headteacher's name is wrong, the address is wrong or, worst of all, you apply for a vacant post at a neighbouring school! Sending an application or letter in an electronic version that you have adapted without having saved all the changes may mean that your letter arrives with all the changes still apparent from the 'tracking' facility of your wordprocessor. It is understood that people often apply for other posts – the issue isn't that, more that you haven't taken sufficient time and trouble to check the final state of your application.

5 Writing a CV

A CV is not always required because of the nature of the application form. A note of caution – if you are not asked for a CV, don't send one because it will normally not be looked at. Personal computers make producing a CV comparatively straightforward. There are even packages designed to help you construct one. There is no set structure for a CV but it should contain the information shown in Table 2.7.

TABLE 2.7   A model CV

- Personal details – name, address, telephone, e-mail, NI number, teacher's number.
- Current post – the title and main responsibilities. It is a nice touch to include your key areas of strength and significant achievements to date.
- Recent courses and professional development.
- Recent projects and initiatives.
- Qualifications – degree, A levels etc.
- Teaching history.
- Referees.

There are other headings that could be included such as hobbies and interests, employment outside teaching etc. The headings are a personal choice. Your CV should be updated regularly and should be easily tailored to the demands of particular applications.

Many application forms are in electronic form. This makes it easier to fill them out and to amend but this can lead to mistakes of the kind where you apply for a job at another school. It is better to type than write because it is clearer and will photocopy better than a handwritten version. The information required is usually similar to that in the list above. Some forms ask you to write your letter of application in a given space. Many schools under local authority control require the application form so that your salary can be assessed by the relevant department. It is important that the information you give is accurate and that any gaps in your career are explained.

Your letter and application form have to be honest – you will normally have to sign them to declare that the information is correct. Exaggerating or lying about your work or qualifications is simply not worth the risk – it may give you an initial marginal advantage but if you are found out it can lead to dismissal. Schools will ask you for proof of your qualifications – so it is vital that the record you give is genuine.

6   Sending the covering letter and application from

A covering letter should be used whenever there is just an application form. It should be addressed to the headteacher and state that you are applying for the named post and that you include a completed application form.

Such a letter is important not only because of etiquette but also because it enables a busy headteacher to focus on the purpose of your letter. In a large school it is not unusual for there to be up to 20 teaching posts vacant each year. Popular schools can attract up to 100 applications for a promoted post and anything which makes the task straightforward for the school will be welcomed.

When your application is ready, ask someone to check it over to make sure that it is free from mistakes. Make sure that you tell your current headteacher that you are making the application – this sometimes gets forgotten, and it doesn't get the process off to a good start if the request for a reference is received without your head expecting it. If you are applying for a post at a local school then it is not unusual for headteachers to discuss applications at meetings and in conversation. Headteachers don't like it if they are asked about applications that they know nothing about!

Ensure that you post the application in good time, with the correct amount of postage. It is good advice to pay for it yourself and not to use the school post. When heads receive envelopes that have clearly been taken from school stationery and franked with the school's postage mark it looks bad. It is misuse of school resources and some headteachers will reject an application on this basis, as a point of principle.

7 Interview preparation and etiquette

The timetable for the selection day will vary from school to school but will include some of the events given in Table 2.8 – it also provides notes and comments on each event.

8 Questions to consider

The purpose of the interview is to assess whether you are the right person for the school. Having written a successful letter of application, which has been supported by your referee, the interview is the main method for selecting the successful applicant. There are a number of general points concerning technique to consider before we discuss the questions normally asked:

■ Use names where possible.

■ Answer questions concisely.

TABLE 2.8 Selection day events with notes and comments

Event	Notes	Comments
Introduction by the headteacher	▪ This is so that the headteacher can meet the candidates and tell them a little about the school and the programme for the day. ▪ This meeting rarely forms part of the selection procedure.	▪ Usually a very pleasant part of the day. ▪ There may be the opportunity for questions but you should not try to overimpress with big questions. ▪ Dress appropriately – this is the first impression you will make.
Tour of the school, often guided by pupils	▪ This gives candidates an insight into the school at work. ▪ Pupils may be asked for feedback on how the candidates responded. ▪ This is to see if you are observant.	▪ A possible question at interview is to comment on something you have observed on the tour.
Visit to the department/ faculty/team area	▪ How do you relate to members of the team? ▪ What do you ask to see? ▪ What questions do you ask? ▪ What information do you find out?	▪ This may include a talk with the present incumbent.
Making a presentation	You will be tested on: ▪ presenting your ideas to an audience ▪ personal presence ▪ doing a presentation to time ▪ response to questions from the audience.	▪ Try to inspect the venue beforehand. ▪ Check to see if you can use an OHP or flip-chart. ▪ If appropriate, produce handouts – but distribute them at the end of the presentation. ▪ Answer the audience, not just the person asking the question.

TABLE 2.8 (cont'd)

Event	Notes	Comments
Writing a paper	You will be tested on: ■ your ability to communicate ■ the clarity of your thinking ■ how you engage with others.	■ Try to keep the paper short – one side of A4 is usually enough. ■ The format of aims, rationale, implementation, evaluation is a good one because it enables you to focus on what you think needs to be done, why it's important, how you would develop and how you will secure improvement through your evaluation. ■ A fully articulated research paper isn't required – readers are looking to see if you are grounded in the practicalities of school life and can transfer your thinking to a school scenario.
Leading a meeting	■ You will be tested on your skills to facilitate a discussion – how you relate to your colleagues.	■ Think about listening rather than speaking. ■ At the start, propose an agenda or process for the discussion – this might be a brainstorm, inviting someone to share. ■ Make sure that you involve everyone – look for clues indicating that people want to contribute. ■ Watch the time to ensure that you don't run over – a good tip for a 15-minute discussion is to summarise the discussion every five minutes or so and agree the next steps.
You may be asked to teach a lesson	■ Your skill as a classroom practitioner will be 'under scrutiny.	■ Show what you can do. Show how much you enjoy teaching your subject. Show that you like teaching children. ■ Consider the OfSTED criteria for a successful lesson – schools will often invite the subject adviser or the link adviser to assist them in the selection process.
Lunch	■ Usually with staff, but may be in the school cafeteria. In primary schools and special schools, lunch will usually be with the children. ■ This is to see how you behave out of class.	■ It is important to appreciate that you are on show all the time. ■ In some schools, anyone who comes into contact with a candidate gives feedback to the panel. This can include lunchtime supervisors, crossing patrol staff etc.

- Do not rush into an answer, pause for thought. The time you spend thinking may seem an age to you, but you will give a more considered answer as a result.

- Give examples based on your experience.

- Try to pick up on things you have learnt about the school.

- Conclude the answer and then stop.

The questions asked at an interview for a middle management position are designed to test your ability to lead and manage a team.

TASK 9

Interview questions

1 Write three bullet points for each response to the questions in Table 2.9.

2 Which criteria from the person specification and job description does each question test?

TABLE 2.9   Interview questions

Question

- Why should pupils learn your subject?

- What are the strengths/weaknesses of the subject team?

- What strategies do you have for improving results at Key Stage X?

- You are appointed today – in a year's time how would you know if you had done a good job?

- What do you look for in a successful lesson?

- How would you assert your authority?

- How would you support a member of your team who teaches disruptive pupils?

- When monitoring the marking of your team, you discover that one teacher has not marked the books for a term. What would you do?

- You receive a complaint from a parent about a teacher in your team. The parent says the teacher has lost some GCSE coursework. The teacher says he gave it back to the pupil. What do you do?

9   Accepting the post

Some schools do not notify candidates of the results of their application until the successful applicant has been offered the post. Other schools phone people with the result very quickly. The offer is a firm contract, although it may be subject to police checks and the like. Therefore, in accepting the job you are entering into and accepting the contract.

It is a great feeling to be given the job you have striven for. The challenges are now firmly ahead of you, but you can be secure in your knowledge that you have thought carefully about the issues underpinning the role. You can be pleased with your appointment because, in making your application in the manner described in this chapter, the school has appointed you for your strengths. You need to be honest in any application. It is bad advice to try to be what they want – it is always better to be yourself. In that way, everyone can be secure in the decision they have made.

————— Summary —————

At the end of this chapter, it is our intention that you will:

- have considered the core purpose of a subject leader
- have a perspective on the function of education, the nature of educational provision and what it means to be a professional teacher
- have considered your motives for wanting promotion
- know the ways in which you can find out about promoted posts
- be able to analyse information about a school and, in particular, the person and job specifications
- create a job application – including a CV and a letter of application
- prepare for an interview for a middle management post.

New suits and a vision

– starting out as a middle manager

Introduction

Starting out on a new role is a very exciting time, but can be one of uncertainty. In many cases, although you will have experience of working alongside others, this will be the first time that you will be 'in charge'. One of the features and challenges of leadership and management in schools is that it operates in layers – a classroom teacher will have a head of department as their manager, but also will be managed by a head of year (as a tutor), and also senior members of staff who have whole school responsibilities. The complexity of school structures can be considerable and the interrelationships between groups and individuals requires sensitivity and awareness. We have called this chapter 'New suits and a vision' because it deals with the first few weeks and months of being a middle manager.

Appointment

In the previous chapter we discussed the application and interview processes and stressed the importance of articulating your views and opinions honestly. This will now become of real importance. The application process is designed to enable the headteacher and governors to decide which of the candidates is right to lead the team. In appointing somebody they are demonstrating their confidence in that person.

In the previous chapter we emphasised the need to 'be yourself' at the interview and to ensure that the opinions you gave were your own and not an attempt to second-guess the school's own agenda. When considering the first few months of the job, it is important to refer back to the principles you articulated in the appointment process.

Securing a middle management post is a cause for celebration. A middle manager has great influence in the development of a subject, or the welfare of the pastoral team or the section of the school under charge. The responsibility is great but there are people whose support you can engage making the task less onerous.

After the celebrations are over there is, for most, a time of realisation when the question arises 'What have I done?' For a teacher this is perhaps more of an issue than in other occupations. School life can be all consuming and it is likely that you will have to leave a school in which you are already a strong and successful teacher to take up the promotion. Good teachers enjoy working with the pupils in their care – many teachers become fond of their pupils and have a close relationship with them. It is not easy to walk away from a group of children who like you, enjoy working for you and with you, and to step out into the unknown, to an alien environment where everyone knows everyone except for you. This may be overstating the case, but there is for all teachers some element of regret on leaving a school. The rhythm of the school year and the nature of the appointment process means that you will have been at the school you are leaving for some time – perhaps a number of years. The stress of this change needs to be acknowledged. This is perhaps at its sharpest for those who leave their first school – leaving your first teaching post (unless it has been awful!) is an emotional experience because this is the school where you began your career and took your first steps in developing your teaching.

However, you have new challenges ahead and, once you have come to terms with leaving the school, you must turn your attention to the new organisation. It is important to disengage from the current school in order to focus on the new role. This process happens naturally as the time comes to an end. Telling children that you are leaving is an important step. However, it is worth taking the advice of senior staff as to when the children are told.

It is very important that you tell the headteacher of your success as soon as possible. If your interview is on a Friday the head will appreciate being called before the end of the school day – if a successor is to be appointed then the deadline for advertisements may be midday on Monday, and being told first thing on a Monday doesn't give much time to draw up an advertisement. It's also vital that you tell your line manager. It's very hurtful to have supported someone in their career to learn of their success via the staffroom grapevine – particularly as your line manager will usually have given a reference for you. A courtesy that is much appreciated, but rarely followed, is to thank your referees for their help and informing them of your success. Writing references takes a great deal of time and it is appropriate to thank those who have supported your application.

You will need to resign from your current school. The offer that is made to you at interview (or thereafter on the telephone, or whatever) is legally binding on both your part and the school's part. Some people prefer to wait for the offer to be confirmed in writing before resigning, but there should be no difficulty in doing so before then (it is useful to mention this to your headteacher as well). Table 3.1 is an example resignation letter.

TABLE 3.1 An example of a resignation letter

---

53 Hampton Road

Limewater

Wilts

31 March 2006

Mrs Fiona Evans

Headteacher

Glatter School

Dear Fiona

Thank you for acting as a referee for my application for the post of Head of Botany at the Kerry Academy.

As I informed you on Friday afternoon, I am delighted to have been successful and I have accepted the post. I would like to offer my resignation from my current post at Glatter School with effect from 31 August 2006.

I understand that you want to advertise my current post and would respectfully remind you that I have not received the formal offer in writing from the Kerry Academy yet.

Yours sincerely

Felix Granville

It is normal practice to visit your new school prior to taking up the position, but there is no right to paid leave of absence for this purpose. Most headteachers will allow this as paid leave, if only because they rely on other schools doing the same. However, if you have been appointed close to the resignation dates (i.e. two months before the end of the term) then it may be difficult to appoint your successor in the intervening period. It may be, therefore, that your Headteacher will be reluctant to release you, particularly if examination classes are going to be affected. If you can anticipate this before asking permission then this will go a long way to smoothing ruffled feathers – headteachers can get quite upset if a person leaves a set of exam classes with no prospect of finding a replacement teacher in the intervening period!

What to tell the children in your classes is a very important consideration. Decide with your line manager when your classes will be told – it may be worth waiting until your successor is appointed. Then you can say 'At the end of this term I am leaving the school and next term you will be taught by Mr X'.

This whole sequence of events is important because your colleagues will remember you in a more favourable light if you observe these niceties. Further, in the future you may wish to apply to the school for a reference, or even for another post at that school. More importantly, however, it is about adopting a professional stance and acting correctly and with propriety. For the children in the class, the prospect of a new teacher can bring feelings of insecurity. This is particularly the case for those who are preparing for public examinations. To be able to say who the new teacher will be demonstrates your lasting commitment to them and shows your control over the situation. In some cases, however, there may be disciplinary difficulties if children believe that their teacher is leaving. There is no easy answer to this problem – children are surprisingly clever at finding out this sort of thing. They are adept at overhearing conversations, and then rumours begin. You are then in a difficult position – should you deny the rumours? It is always ill advised to lie to children – the trust that exists, of necessity, between a teacher and child is easily lost in the face of an obvious untruth.

Having told classes of your departure, your best defence is to carry on as normal. It is important to maintain the standards of discipline and to continue as if you were staying. This will maintain the quality of relationships and avoid any difficulties. Further, you still have responsibility for the class and it is your professional responsibility to maintain standards. If the appointment is for a September start there may be period of several months before you take up the post.

Continuing to work hard with classes and behaving as normal, will, in many cases, put the fact that the teacher is leaving out of the children's minds. Further, in settling matters at school you are ensuring that your classes are passed to the new teacher with minimum disruption to the children's education. This is professional responsibility.

_____ Visiting the new school _____

Having begun the process of disengaging from the school and preparing for the new role, you need to arrange a visit to the new school. For the most part, schools will release a teacher for at least a day. However, if more time is required then the new school may be asked to pay for supply costs to cover the absence. It is important to negotiate these details with both headteachers to facilitate a smooth transition and minimise any disquiet. The visit to the new school will be important because it will be your first chance to meet the team and start to learn about the job that you will be doing. There are several tasks which you need to undertake before visiting the new school.

Using data to inform planning

Setting targets is one thing – hitting them is quite another. If a target is to be properly challenging – i.e. it isn't just a best guess of what the student will achieve anyway – then some students are going to need additional help to ensure they meet them. The debate with colleagues responsible for those students must be moved away from rationalising why they are unlikely to hit the target and towards a determination of actions necessary for them to realise the target.

Critically, the whole thing rests on proper information. Students must be accurately assessed and the assessment information gathered and analysed. Students who are underperforming must be identified and action must be taken to ensure that the underperformance is corrected.

Systems are all important in this. It is no good, from a whole-school point of view, leaving it up to every individual to act, or not act, depending on how they feel about it. The system must include the following steps.

1 Gathering assessment data according to a policy.

2 Comparison with target grades – if the policy is correct then this should produce useful information. If you find that every query raised is explained away by the teacher or head of department saying, 'well this or that hasn't been accounted for' then the assessment reporting policy needs to be revisited. It is essential that all data gathered must be on the same basis and therefore provide comparability.

3 Analysis must be carried out to identify those who are underperforming. This should be carried out at the level of the individual class, department and whole school.

4 Teachers of underperforming students must engage in a discussion of the reasons for the underperformance – what are the barriers to achievement for each individual?

5 Actions must be determined at the level of the class teacher (the most important level), department and whole school.

6 The cycle should repeat at some appropriate level of frequency. This will depend on the age group of the pupils (generally assessment data is gathered more frequently for GCSE students than KS3), the level of need in the school, the other priorities the school has and, the effectiveness of IT-based systems to support the process.

The first step, however, is to identify the areas of underachievement and to analyse where the issues lie.

As an 'outsider' a relatively straightforward step is to look at GCSE data and compare this with the other departments.

Figures 3.1 and 3.2 shows the performance of various departments at a successful school.

TASK 10

Using data to structure planning

You have just been appointed Head of Maths to Fullan School. It is a successful school with 65% of 5 grade A*–C as its benchmark. The proportion of A*/A grades is shown in Figure 3.2.

Prepare for the first meeting with the team.

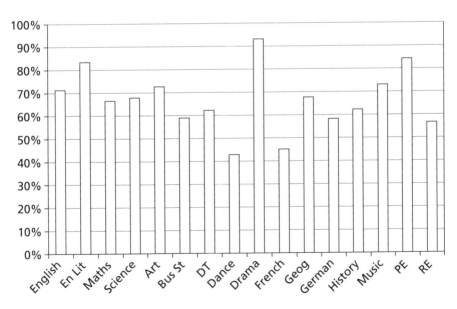

FIG. 3.1   Cumulative grades (%) A*–C by subject

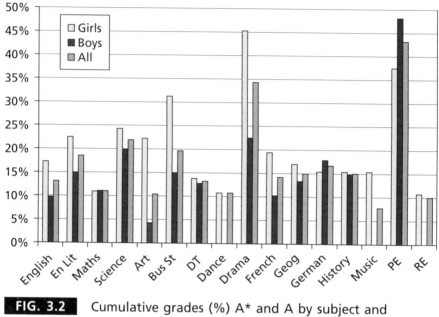

FIG. 3.2   Cumulative grades (%) A* and A by subject and by gender

Preparing for a meeting with the headteacher

This will be the first meeting with the headteacher since your appointment and it is important that you make a positive impression. The headteacher will want to be sure that you have made the right choice in accepting the appointment. By presenting yourself as well organised and focused on the task ahead, you will make good progress in maintaining the positive impression.

TASK 11

Preparing for initial meetings (1)

This task is designed to help you to plan for meeting with the headteacher and in constructing an agenda for the meeting.

You are preparing to visit your new school and you will be having a short meeting with the headteacher.

Prepare an agenda for this 30-minute meeting.

If you prepare an agenda for this meeting this will demonstrate to your new headteacher a well-organised and committed approach. If you are able to send the agenda to the headteacher in advance this will be welcomed and will further underline your control over the role that you are taking on.

A change in staff is an important time for everyone involved. However well you may compare with your predecessor (even if they were a complete disaster!) there are always uncertainties about how the new person will settle in and whether they will be happy and successful. It doesn't matter if your predecessor was wonderful or terrible – the anxieties the school will have will be the same. If the former, the concern will be rooted very much in whether the progress of the team will continue. If the latter then the concern will be whether you will be able to do the difficult job you have taken on. Well-organised people are great to work with because school managers will be reassured and won't have to worry.

The agenda should include some ideas on what you think needs to be tackled initially. If you are able to give some idea of your first meeting with the team then this will not only add to the headteacher's positive view but also give the head the opportunity to offer guidance and support. There are people in schools who are unwilling to share with the headteacher or members of the leadership team, somehow thinking that to do so exposes them to criticism. This should not be the case – it is really important that you give the headteacher sufficient information about what you intend to do. If you think to yourself 'this is too trivial to bother the head with' then resist that for the first few conversations – the head will soon tell you if it's information they don't need to know. However, it is better to be told this than to be caught out by not sharing the necessary information.

As you articulate your proposals and ideas for the first few weeks, avoid being too ambitious. Starting out at a new school is like starting a new job. All the things that are familiar to you are gone. Having built up, over a period of time, a body of knowledge about how your current school runs (where to go, who to see and what to do) and knowing lots of children's names, and them knowing you and your ways, when you go to a new school you have to start again. The relaxed manner you may have cultivated over five years may be interpreted as weakness by your new classes. Gone are the days when new classes used to be very quiet with a new teacher, before testing the boundaries. In many schools teachers have a difficult time for the first few weeks and months establishing themselves with new classes. The priority as you begin your new job must be with your classes and your new colleagues. It is impossible to have an impact as a middle manager if you are struggling with your own teaching.

The objectives of this meeting are to begin the induction process and to engage support. By articulating your priorities for the first few weeks, you are confirming the wisdom of your appointment. It is vital for the future success of your team that such an initial meeting is planned. You may be concerned. The headteacher will normally want to guide you and want to offer advice and support. This is particularly important when leading a team where there have been difficulties. For the new middle manager, it is crucial that you consider very carefully what advice you are offered – only a very confident person neglects guidance!

You need to have considered carefully your priorities for those first few weeks. There is something of a dilemma to be faced here. At the start of a new job, you are likely to be bursting with ideas and full of enthusiasm – this is certainly desirable, if not essential. There will, of course, be a measure of nervousness and anxiety at the prospect of the fresh challenge. The balance that has to be struck is between trying to achieve too much in the first weeks and failing to make a positive impression. You have been appointed because of your ideas, and the belief that you have the skills to lead the team to higher standards of achievement. However, a team takes time to build and there is an opportunity to achieve goals but in a planned and measured manner.

Your first priorities will include:

- learning your way around the school
- learning the systems of the school
- establishing yourself with classes
- getting to know the team
- beginning to bring about change.

The balance is a difficult one because everyone will be looking at you to see what you do in the first few weeks. Members of the team will have some anxieties because of the uncertainty that any change brings about. A clear agenda will be useful at this stage.

TASK 12

Preparing for initial meetings (2)

A team meeting is scheduled for the end of the school day on which you are making your initial visit to the school. In the letter arranging the visit it is suggested that you lead this meeting.

Prepare an agenda for this meeting

Having a new boss is a time of uncertainty – people's concerns may manifest themselves in a number of ways including resistance, overfamiliarity, hostility, reticence and many other behaviours. This first meeting is, therefore, a very important one – the impression you want to create with your new team is critical. The best advice we can give is to 'be yourself' and to avoid making huge generalisations because this is a very good way to wind people up and create resentment. A good maxim is to listen more than you talk.

The agenda

Having a published agenda will help set the scene for the meeting. If you have a second in department then involving that person will be a good move. Not only will it support you in the first few weeks and months but it will also show that you are committed to working together. In addition, it takes some of the pressure off you at that first meeting.

1 Introductions – If this is the first time you have met the team since the appointment, some introductions are necessary as they may not remember you (or indeed you them). You may have met all of the team at the interview, but they may not remember all that much about you. This is not from disrespect but it was a working day for them, and they will have met the other candidates too!

2 Your philosophy – Your new colleagues will want to know something about you. They will be interested in your background, your current school and some idea of your views on subject (if appropriate) or pupil matters. For a subject team it is important that the leader has a view on the purpose of the subject. It is important to state this clearly, but if it is at variance with what you have found out about the team, the statement needs to be tempered. If, as a result of your analysis of the school or conversations you have had, you know that a radical change will be required then taking advice from the head or a senior member of staff will help to shape your presentation of the changes you are looking to introduce.

3 Your principles – Without sounding too pompous, it's really important to say how you want to work with the team. The team needs to know how you will work with them – there may be uncertainties over this and your statement will give direction and help to address insecurities. The balance here is between your role as a middle manager and as a teacher. It is important to appreciate the role and its implications.

4 The first project – All eyes will be on you and therefore it is a good thing to have something that you plan to do that involves the whole team. You should choose a project in which you are confident, and which does not depend heavily on the skills of the team but still provides an opportunity for the team to enjoy success in a joint endeavour. The best project is one where the case for action is unarguable and one that matches people's concerns. Using your analysis will be useful data to discuss with the group.

Having prepared for such a meeting the outcome will be that you have:

- introduced yourself to the team

- started to get to know the team

- articulated your philosophy

- begun the process of managing the team, by stating your principles – these are inviolate statements which you can refer to as time goes on

- emphasised your management capability by setting up a small-scale project which will enable you to work with the team.

You will probably be nervous about the outcome of this meeting. The first meeting with a new group is always a challenge. It may even be the first meeting you have chaired. However, by deciding the format and the outcomes, the challenge will be made easier.

The actual timing of the meeting is relevant here. All schoolteachers are subject to *directed time*. The Teachers' Pay and Conditions Document (STPCD) is published each year by the Secretary of State for Education. This sets out the pay scale and the determining factors to be applied in deciding the point on the scale at which any teacher in a particular post will start. It also sets out in significant detail the conditions of employment, specifying the directed time of 1265 hours per year that a teacher must be available to work under the direction of the headteacher, and the duties that are to be performed both within and outside the directed time. For the most part, meetings of this kind will count as directed time. Hence, the meeting may be specified to last one hour, for example. It is important, therefore, that the meeting does not overrun. It will demonstrate good managerial skill if the meeting is controlled in such a way that it is effectively chaired and sensitively managed to finish on time. Some people like to put their watch in front of them to help them to gauge the time accurately – others will decide, in advance, the amount of time to be spent on particular items on the agenda and arrange the meeting accordingly. In planning this first meeting, it is worthwhile checking if there are any other matters which need to be dealt with. If the meeting only occurs as part of a five- or six-week cycle, then it is likely that there are important procedural and administrative matters to address.

Getting to know everyone

The first few days of the new job are likely to be stressful but also, in our experience, very pleasant. They will be stressful because there is so much with which to become acquainted. Moving from a position in which you know everyone and are fully conversant with all the systems to one where everything is unfamiliar is very stressful. The learning you have to do is heightened by the need to become established in the new role. However, while expectations of you may be high (that is why you have been appointed) there is a recognition that it does take time for people to settle in before they can be at their most effective.

Your priorities in your first few days in the role of middle manager are:

- getting to know the team and their strengths and weaknesses
- getting to know the team as teachers
- establishing yourself with your classes (still the most important thing!)
- getting to know the staff.

Getting to know your team

Your first priority is to learn about the staff in your team. This is vital if the team is to make progress and you are to manage them effectively. Some managers may wish to have individual meetings with each member of the team and conduct some sort of fact-finding exercise. If there is the time to do this, it can be a very useful and efficient way in which to set the tone for the future workings of the team. If, however, the nature of the school or the team is contrary to this method of working, you will have to decide whether this is the most suitable way of getting to know the team.

TASK 13

Finding out about your team

1 Think about the kind of information you need to find out.
2 Think also about the kind of response you might anticipate from individual teachers.

3 Consider how you will respond to hostility or indifference. If there are particular management issues within the team (for example, incompetence, long-term grievances etc.) how will you manage these within the context of this interview process?

A good place to start is the *'how long have you been teaching here'* question. This will give you a good insight into the profile of the team and the blend of experience the team has. It is important to think about how you will deal with the 'too long' response. Similarly, if you decide to ask how long people have been teaching then dealing with some cynicism or a maudlin comment takes some skill. At this stage, it is often good advice to accept the comment and when you know the person better then return to the remark.

Asking about the teacher's academic background can be beneficial but sometimes people are a little reluctant to talk about this. Another way of tackling it is to ask people how they come to be teaching at the school and to get some background on their career path. Finding out about people's university or college time will give you some further ideas on how the team can be developed – for example, you might discover that a member of staff has a computer studies qualification in addition to their main degree.

Finding ways to listen rather than talk is the way forward when getting to know a new team. So, if all else fails then ask about the classes that a person is teaching this year. This is a useful question to ask because most teachers like to talk about their classes. And, of course, it will allow you to ask about specific classes. This is useful if the development required is within a key stage. This can lead into questions about exam results and what the teacher's results for their classes have been over the past three years. Again, many teachers enjoy talking about their classes and asking this will both emphasise the purpose of the meeting and also give the teacher the opportunity to describe their successes, or otherwise.

Finally, ask people what they see as the priorities for the team. This needs to be handled carefully. The responses should reveal the team's views about developments that have been undertaken before. Each teacher can have a say at the outset. You need to be careful that you don't make promises that you cannot, or may not be able to, keep in an attempt to get a relationship off to a good start. Being a principled person is more important than being popular.

By collecting this body of information you will have started to form views on the priorities for the team, and indeed the capacity that the team has to bring about improvement. Although the description of the team has so far been about teachers, many teams now include teaching assistants, technicians and other support staff. It is vital that when you meet with individual teachers that you include other team members – otherwise they will feel very left out – you will also miss out on vital information that they have.

Putting this information together will give you a team profile and this could be created as follows.

Creating a team profile

The team profile is very much about answering the following questions.

- What is the balance within the team? Gender, experience, time at the school, academic background? Are there training needs?

- Monitoring of teachers' work – has the experience been a positive one (for example, how did the team cope and respond to OfSTED?) and have the issues raised been addressed?

- Are the results from the team in line with expectations? What do teachers expect? What use is made of benchmark data?

- What is the team's response to change? Does it see the need for change? Is the change you have planned anticipated?

- Is the team cohesive and coherent? How have they responded to this fact finding? Is the issue of team building an urgent one? How will the team respond to being managed? Are there difficulties with your management style adopted at this early stage?

These are important questions which need to be answered. The results of these discussions will enable you to compile a profile of the team under the following headings.

1 What are the issues for development?

2 What further information do you need before deciding what to focus on?

3 What are the key people in the team who will be able to lead the development?

4 Who will be passive or resist the proposed development?

Having a team profile enables you to decide how to start to lead the team. Of course, this process can be tailored to meet the culture of the school. Schools which are run very much on a business model would welcome this approach. However, a small village school, where the manager is a subject coordinator, may find this approach too radical and any attempt to conduct this kind of interview may be met with strong resistance. The well-meant objective may be scuppered by how people react to your management style. This is a health warning for all managers in schools. The rationale and the process may be absolutely sound, but if the cultural change is too great, the process will not be successful in the long term and the manager's job will be more difficult the next time around.

This issue illustrates the dilemma of school management. While one person is charged with leading a team and having responsibility for the tasks that are set, successful schools work on the basis of cooperation and a commitment to teamwork. Teachers are not proletarians who can be told to do things in a certain way. While they can be directed to perform certain tasks, subversion (to give it the most pejorative name) is practised widely in schools because of the isolated nature of the teaching process. This issue will be discussed in greater depth in Chapter 4.

Getting to know the team as teachers

In order to bring about improvements to the quality of teaching, you will need to have a view on the quality of teaching and learning within the team. While the OfSTED report – where it exists – is a useful source of information, you need to assess teaching and learning for yourself. You can organise a programme of lesson observation over a period of time and this will have the effect of emphasising your quality control function. Of course, as a new manager you have a good reason for wanting to undertake this process – simply because you are new. However, in the bid to establish yourself with your own classes, you need to plan the lesson observations with some care. Taking time out of your own teaching to go and observe a colleague may be the only way in which you can achieve the objective – but is something to be avoided in the first period. Engaging the help of a senior member of staff, or perhaps the second in the department, is a good way forward.

How you manage the period of lesson observation is critical to its success and will depend a great deal on how it is used in the school already. If you join a school where lesson observation is firmly embedded in the culture of staff development then most people will probably expect you to get involved in this. Some schools, particularly those who use the OfSTED model, have well-developed policies that mean that lesson observation can only be undertaken after a period of training. If you read the staff handbook and talk to a senior colleague or a fellow team leader then this will help you to get this right. Lesson observation can arouse strong emotions in people and it is important to at least know the shared view of this before embarking on a programme that might be regarded as autocratic, or indeed lightweight.

A useful way of beginning the dialogue on the quality of teaching and learning is to establish with the team:

- that the purpose of lesson observation, at this stage, is for you to gain information about the teaching strengths of the team
- that you will make the criteria for the lesson observation clear to all
- that you will give feedback from the lesson observation
- that, where possible, teachers can choose which class you observe.

The purpose of this procedure is to be open and honest with the team. The teachers may still have anxieties about the new regime and this approach leaves no room for anyone to suggest a hidden agenda for the observations. The criteria for lesson observation should be clearly stated and should be fairly bland at this stage. Much can be gained by observing the relationship between the teacher and the class.

As an opening strategy, the criteria for these lesson observations could be:

- the quality of relationships between teacher and pupils
- how the teacher introduces the work to the class
- how much time is spent on tasks during the lesson
- how the tasks are differentiated
- the link between classwork and homework.

There are a number of other criteria which could be substituted in this list, but the objective of the observation needs to be kept in mind. The purpose is to enable you to construct a profile of the teaching in the team. Depending on the situation, you might choose to develop a set of criteria for this first set of observations, or to simply use the existing school systems. We recommend that if there is a system already then that should be used to start with and then talk about changing it as a result of the observations. As part of the feedback to the teacher, both you and the teacher could use the pro forma shown in Table 3.2.

TABLE 3.2 Teacher observation feedback pro forma	
Lesson evaluation	**Response**
■ How did you link the lesson with previous and future learning?	
■ Did you explain and illustrate clearly what you expected pupils to achieve by the end of the lesson?	
■ How did you communicate your expectations to the pupils?	
■ Did all the pupils behave appropriately during the lesson?	
■ What strategies did you use to ensure this?	
■ What teaching strategies did you use and how effective were they?	
■ What questioning techniques did you use?	
■ What activities did you think were successful in your lesson?	
■ What criteria did you use to assess success?	
■ What work did the pupils produce in the lesson? How will you assess it?	
■ What homework did you set for this class? How will you assess it?	
■ If you planned this lesson again, how would you plan it differently?	

The benefits of such a pro forma are that, at this stage, the criteria for the evaluation are not particularly contentious and involve the teacher in the act. This is important when establishing a dialogue with the teacher to discuss their work. It is vital, in these early stages, to create a forum where the quality of teaching and learning are discussed in an open and honest way and that you are seen as proactive and yet supportive. There may be a time when you have to assert yourself and act as a disciplinary agent, but if this process is not to be compromised you should avoid it at this stage.

An additional priority in the first few days is to establish yourself with your classes. You will need to be a highly effective classroom practitioner and you set the standard for the rest of the team. It is part of the management function to set standards and these will be compromised if you are found wanting in any respect. However, you are not a superhero and you need to bear this in mind. Certainly there are some aspects of the job in which there is no compromise on standards. These include:

- preparation for class
- quality of teaching
- quality of assessment and marking
- consistency of behaviour management.

However, this is not to say that you will never get things wrong. Every leader needs to have a measure of humility and be prepared to own up to both the enormity of the task and the impossibility of perfection. However, you cannot be found wanting when the issues concern the standards of teaching and learning. This is the professional manager.

You can use your interactions with your own classes to establish yourself in the school. By focusing on the quality of teaching and learning, and demonstrating effective and consistent behaviour management, the pupils will become aware of the efficacy of the methods. Gone are the days when pupils lived in fear of their teacher, but there will be times when you have to pick up the pieces of a failing relationship between pupil and teacher. As time goes on, behaviour management may become an issue for the team and there will need to be a full discussion on the team approach.

You will occupy a pivotal role in the life of the team and the development of the subject or pastoral team. You will also be a member of the school staff – this is discussed fully in Chapter 5. It is important to recognise that while you are the leader of the team, it is not the only team in the school and that there are others who have a similar role. Further, in secondary schools the middle manager leading a subject will normally be a form tutor and as such be part of a pastoral team – and the pastoral leader will be part of a subject team. In a primary school, a coordinator will also be a class teacher and so on. This point is made to illustrate the interdependency of the teaching staff, and as such the new middle manager needs to spend time getting to know all their colleagues. In addition, there are the ancillary staff with whom the manager will interact – they are important to the life of the school and positive relationships need to be cultivated. There is no hiding the fact that the first few weeks and months of middle management are characterised by hard work and persistent interaction with pupils and staff. However, over time the relationships which the teacher cherished at the previous school will be replaced by good relationships built up at the new school. This is the induction process for the middle manager.

Dealing with a team member who also applied for your job

In some cases you will have to work with a member of your team who also applied for the job. This can be very difficult and there are several factors to consider.

■ In the main, any resentment will not be direct towards you, because it is not your fault! Most teachers recognise this. Any resentment or hostility will come from hurt pride or a failure of senior management to debrief the teacher adequately.

■ It is worthwhile, therefore, asking the headteacher how this teacher responded to the debrief and to seek advice.

■ The teacher may be watchful and wary – some may watch to see if you fail. The sensitive middle manager acknowledges the hurt and treats the teacher with courtesy, but is also guarded. Your processes and interactions will need to be proper. This is not only for their own sake, but also to obviate any sense of 'could have done better'.

■ If the teacher is serious about promotion you can help them, in a sensitive manner, to prepare for such a role. This needs to be undertaken with care.

In general, teachers are accommodating people who recognise one another's strengths. If you are to be successful, you will have to prove yourself to all – this includes the headteacher, senior management, team members (supportive or otherwise), other staff, pupils, parents and so on. By demonstrating an awareness of feelings and a sensitive approach, you will already have learnt a valuable lesson in people management.

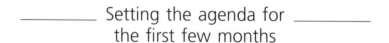

Setting the agenda for the first few months

The objectives of the first few weeks are to give yourself the opportunity to get to know the team and to establish yourself both as the leader and as a teacher. However, as time goes on you will wish, and be expected, to set an agenda for the changes you will bring about. The reason why it is important to wait before embarking on a major change is that until you know the strengths of the team, the development you lead will be yours alone. By getting to know the strengths of the team, you can use their interests as a means of engaging support.

There is one situation, however, where it is impossible to wait. This is in the case of a failing school or failing subject area. Under these circumstances, you are dealing directly with the headteacher and will not be given the comparative luxury of getting to know the team before you act. In this case you need to be very clear on your purpose and be sure of your methods. In many ways the methods are the same – they rely on a leader with a clearly articulated philosophy who acts in a principled manner. However, if the team is hostile to you then the sharing of your philosophy at that opening meeting may have to be tempered, or even saved for another occasion.

You may have no choice about the actions you have to take. However, in the long term, decisive and assertive strategies will have only a limited impact if a principled leader and effective manager does not deliver them. Delivering a difficult message is not an excuse for roughshod treatment of people. It is our view that being assertive and proactive is synonymous with principled leadership. Being horrid and unpleasant is not. There are times when managers have to say unpleasant things. You may have to tell a teacher that their teaching is unsatisfactory and that you may have to be part of capability, competency or disciplinary procedures, but this does not have to be done in an aggressive or unpleasant manner. Avoiding this is the mark of a professional manager.

Taking care of yourself

In these first few months you will be under a good deal of stress. For most people, changing a job is one of the most stressful experiences. It follows closely behind bereavement, divorce and moving house. It is important for the new middle manager to try to avoid additional stresses. While one cannot always predict the events which shape our lives, there are steps we can take to minimise our stress levels.

A crucial factor for most people is the quality of their personal relationships. While it may be tempting to embark on a new phase in one's career when a relationship comes to an end, it will be difficult to sustain oneself and the necessary emotional energy required for the new job if outside of school one's personal life is in tatters. Further, when establishing oneself in a new job it is difficult to know who can be spoken to in confidence – and it is bad for a team's morale if their new manager is emotionally exhausted. It is surely better counsel to delay a new job until the emotional demands are lessened and all one's energy can be devoted to the job.

Similarly, there are events which do fall beyond our control, such as illness and bereavement. But teachers need to consider their lives carefully before embarking on the promotional ladder. Opportunities will be there in the future, and you do yourself no favours by trying to combine the care of a relative, the birth of a baby or moving house with a demanding new job.

When in post you need to take your own health seriously and achieve a balance in your life. It is important to keep healthy, and if playing squash or going to the gym or walking the dog is part of that healthy lifestyle then you need to maintain these activities. Also, it is easy to take health for granted and to neglect oneself in terms of diet, fitness and relaxation. The balance comes from being fit to do the job. Anyone involved in education will appreciate the enormity of the task and that the drive for perfection is never ending. However, by prioritising the needs of pupils, the team and oneself, a balance can be struck. If you really think that you cannot take an hour out to go to the gym, you need to look at how the work is being organised.

There are strategies for balancing the demands of home and school. Some of these include:

- engaging a partner's support and agreeing the division of domestic chores
- paying for a cleaner or other domestic help
- bartering time with friends to organise childcare
- organising reliable childcare
- using the Internet to do the shopping etc.
- planning time to do things such as going to a yoga class, socialising etc. and sticking to it
- joining a club or activity that takes place regularly and therefore you have to leave school every Tuesday at 4.30pm – tell your team that's why you have to go.

All successful middle managers have to make appropriate judgements and compromise their personal and professional lives – it is a question of balance. We can get the things done that we value, and we should value ourselves most highly of all.

How to develop a vision

. . . and how to share it with others, how to develop shared aims, moving from aims to development planning.

Having a vision is quite a difficult thing to describe – and yet it is vital to the development of a team or a subject that the leader has one. Put simply, it's how you want it to look in the future. If you are the head of English, for example, the vision for English in the school is about:

- how it is taught
- what children learn (this could be the emphasis on novels, poetry, drama)
- what English classrooms look like
- how the team works together
- how children are assessed
- how they are rewarded
- whether English is about reading or writing
- the place media studies have in your department
- and so on.

The first thing to note is that developing a vision takes time. It is often the result of critical incidents where you see something happening (for good or for bad) and think about how you would behave in that situation.

The first question to ask is 'How has your subject changed over time and what do you think needs to happen further?' Making a list of the various initiatives that you have been involved in implementing is a good first step – thinking about how children have responded is another. Then think about how your subject will be taught, and how it will look in say, ten years time.

The second question to ask is about the learning environment – what do you think a good learning environment is like? Do children sit in rows, in groups? What is on the walls of the classrooms and what is in the classrooms (computers, data projectors, whiteboards, books)? Do the children work in all-ability groups or in ability sets? What's the rationale for both of these?

The third question is how your team will work together. Do you see yourself as the head of department, the coordinator or the leader of the team? How you intend to work with the team is a really important issue to consider. If you believe that everyone has an equal contribution to make and that you are happy for others to lead on projects then the way you conduct yourself in meetings will need to reflect this.

By asking these questions in a team meeting you can start to develop shared aims. Asking 'If children could choose to do our subject, would they do so?' is a challenging but useful starting point. Thinking about what you want children to take away from the subject is the next issue to consider. How you move from the aims to the development plan will be explored in depth in Chapter 7.

Of course department or team aims are no good if they are simply discussed once and never looked at again. By forming aims you set the compass for the future direction of the team's work. Revisiting them regularly is the key to embedding those aims into the way of working.

Leading change

One of the most important aspects of the middle manager's job is to lead effective change.

Change is fundamental to the education process and over recent years could be described as endemic. A classic definition of the change process is a linear model:

$$objectives \rightarrow content \rightarrow organisation \rightarrow evaluation.$$

Put simply, we decide what we want to achieve (i.e. what the objectives are), then decide on how we are going to do it (i.e. what the outcomes will be), then consider the organisation of the objectives (i.e. how we shall do it) and then finally evaluate the exercise. This model has been adapted to become more of a cyclical one – the evaluation is part of the change process in itself and the act of evaluation informs the change process. The change process is also a continuous one and this, in some ways, is the cause of its difficulties in school.

Many schools are engaged in managing multiple changes, and this raises major curriculum planning issues which will need to be considered fully later.

Objectives-based models are, despite their wide use, open to a number of objections because they are considered as mechanistic. There is a feeling that schools do not function in this way. Schools are cultural organisations and change is a difficult thing to bring about. If we are to accept the notion that a school is a cultural organisation, there are several characteristics we need to consider in relation to the change process.

The culture of a school is the way things are done. It goes beyond the outward signs and includes such matters as the attitude to classrooms – are they seen as an individual teacher's space? In some schools the classroom is a named teacher's domain and permission is required to enter. The lesson can be fiercely guarded as an interaction between the teacher and the class, and to observe the lesson requires, again, the seeking of permission. In reality, however, the line manager and the teacher play a game in which the teacher cannot refuse and the line manager does not have to ask – this is the nature of interaction in some schools.

However, one of the main objections to the linear process of change is that a school is an interactive place. It relies on the complex interactions between groups of adults and pupils. The nature of human interaction is such that it is not rigid – it is complex and complicated. Change management needs to acknowledge this and change becomes a process.

Another way of thinking of this linear model is to consider:

- What educational purposes should we seek to achieve?
- What educational experiences can we provide that are likely to achieve these purposes?
- How can these educational experiences be effectively organised?
- How can we determine whether these purposes are being achieved?

The major issue at this level, for the middle manager, is where do these objectives come from? In some cases the objectives derive from benchmark data that suggests that standards need to be raised – but this does not really answer the question. Also, the issue with the evaluative part of the model is that some observable change in behaviour would need to happen before the achievement of the objective. Consequently, all objectives would need to be expressed in behaviour terms rather than educational ones. The point here is that strategic change cannot always be measured in a meaningful way – there are indicators which point to improvement but these, in themselves, may not be accurate measures of the intended outcomes.

For middle managers, the strategic changes they will lead will fall into several categories and these are illustrated in Table 3.3.

Strategic change is not just about setting objectives and organising events and measuring the results – it is a more subtle process. In order

TABLE 3.3 Categories of middle manager-led strategic change

Category	Example	Measures
Skill-based	■ Staff are able to deliver a new aspect of the curriculum – e.g. use ICT as part of the scheme of work in Geography. ■ The school is delivering the numeracy hour.	This could be measured in terms of the actual delivery of ICT, by producing a timetable for the delivery etc. But it is only by a qualitative assessment of the teaching, and sampling of the work produced, that the skill-based strategic change can be assessed.
Performance-based	■ There is an improvement in the pass rate at A level in an FE college. ■ There is an improvement in the reading ages of 5-year old children.	The percentages for each of the subject areas could be compared with previous years' but there is a need to use baseline figures to make any assessment valid. The improvement in pass rate does not necessarily mean that the measures put in place have led to the increase. The manager needs to consider the outcomes with greater care.
Knowledge-based	■ Pupils know how to use the Internet. ■ History pupils know about the consequences of the Napoleonic wars.	These are knowledge-based objectives and can be measured using a test. However, the question arises – how long does a pupil need to retain the knowledge to meet this objective? If the pupil knows the facts at the end of the lesson, is this success? If they are unable to recall the facts the next lesson, is this failure?
Attitude-based	■ Pupils have a positive attitude to attending school.	Attendance figures and truancy rates can be useful, but an attitudinal survey would be needed.
Cultural	■ Pupils are dropping less litter in school. ■ Pupils are wearing a new school uniform. ■ Pupils are choosing to study ICT at GCSE. ■ Pupils are choosing GNVQ at FE college.	Cultural change is difficult to quantify. A manager will not wish to count pieces of litter! The change that is required is the 'feeling that litter should not be dropped' or 'pupils feel proud of their uniform and want to wear it'. This example illustrates the complexity of strategic change.

that strategic change brings about a lasting change, it has to embrace the existing culture of the school and move forward in a planned way. It is not haphazard. However, it recognises that it is people that bring about strategic change. There are several issues we need to consider in this context.

Determining the need for change

How do we determine the need for change? This is quite a hard question to answer, because in some cases it is obvious – improvements in the reading ages of 7-year olds at the school need to be made. However, while a programme which seeks to bring about these improvements can be set up and the outcomes clearly specified, it will not be lasting change unless the features which underpin the change become part of the practice of those who teach reading.

Determining the need for change can be difficult, particularly if you, as the manager, are the only one who recognises this need. It is important, therefore, that as part of the process of leading change that you engage the support of the leadership team in the school or college. It is vital for the success of the change that you are supported. It can be lonely and difficult to lead a change when there is no one following – you need the support and encouragement of your superiors.

Change models

Change has to become part of the custom and practice of the school. In this way the staff and pupils take ownership of the matter. You need to recognise that your role is to lead and manage the change – it is not to do all the work. Your role is visionary in that you see what needs to be done and are able to bring about 'followership' on the part of the team. Your role is also functional, in that you devise a process where the actions are completed and the objectives met.

This can be quite hard to do. However, there are change models which are useful to consider and will form a good basis for strategic planning. The model for strategic change shown in Table 3.4 is based on Gibbons (1977). There are seven major stages in the model – each has its own kind of task, its own kind of process and its own product.

The emphasis here is on a dynamic process which is not intransigent. It is responsive – it is evaluative and is driven by change itself. However, your task is to translate this model into a process that you can use to plan your work.

TABLE 3.4 Model for strategic change

Task	Process	Product
1 *Identify* what job the curriculum has to do.	*Analyse* the situation.	A clear *purpose* for curriculum development.
2 *Formulate* a means of achieving the purpose.	*Design* a curriculum concept.	A promising *theoretical model* of the curriculum.
3 *Select* an appropriate *teaching* strategy for the curriculum.	*Establish* principles of procedure for students anc teachers when using the curriculum.	A specific *teaching/learning* strategy.
4 *Produce* the curriculum delivery system.	*Develop* the means required to present and maintain the curriculum.	An *operational* curriculum.
5 *Experiment* with the curriculum on student learning and the school.	*Refine* the model through classroom research and regular improvements.	A *refined* curriculum.
6 *Implement* the curriculum throughout the school in other settings.	*Change* general practice to the new curriculum.	A *widely used* curriculum.
7 *Evaluate* the effects of the curriculum on student learning.	*Evaluate* how effective the curriculum is.	A *proven* curriculum.

Improving study skills

Louise is Head of Year in a comprehensive school. She is concerned that the children find it difficult to study effectively. As part of the pastoral team Louise has been given the objective of improving study skills for children in the school. She recognises that a change to current practice will be needed to achieve this objective. Table 3.5 sets out her plan for change.

TABLE 3.5 Planning change

Task	Process	Product
1 *Identify*. Here Louise needs to identify what needs to be done and she will be able to do this by finding out about the existing practices and the problems these create. She identifies that an improvement in the ability of children to study is required.	*Analyse*. By conducting some kind of audit of study skills Louise will be able to find out about existing good practice and the outcomes it produces. By examining the demands of the curriculum as a whole she can see where the gaps in this aspect of the curriculum are.	*Purpose*. The purpose for the development is clear – to improve study skills. However, by clear identification of the needs of the children and the issues raised by the deficiencies in the curriculum, the purpose of the development is clarified.
2 *Formulate*. At this stage Louise can work with others to consider a range of possible ways of delivering a study skills programme. She may decide that it should be delivered as part of the tutorial programme or in a cross-curricular mode. However, the formulation of the programme will be	*Design*. By designing an appropriate model for the delivery of study skills based on existing good practice and the needs of the children, Louise embraces the present with the future. This is good practice because it starts	*Theoretical model*. By spending time finding out and planning on the basis of pupil need and curriculum strength, the emphasis for the programme will evolve naturally. By focusing on the strengths and weaknesses, others

TABLE 3.5 *(cont'd)*

Task	Process	Product
facilitated by the information she collected in the identification stage.	from where the school is, and looks forward to where it wants to be.	will be able to work with Louise to develop appropriate teaching strategies.
3 *Teaching strategy*. Louise works with her team to consider how they are going to deliver study skills as part of the tutorial programme. She invites middle managers with curriculum responsibility to join the group to consider how the teaching programme in core subjects can support the study skills programme she is designing.	*Establish*. At this stage the strategic principles for this new curriculum are clear – it is a cross-curricular programme and a tutorial programme delivered so as to support one another. By establishing this at the outset the planning becomes more productive.	A specific teaching/*learning* strategy.
4 *Produce*. Now Louise is able to work with the group to devise teaching programmes. The group uses the needs analysis undertaken at the start and plans around these. Subject representatives will be able to commit their teams to supporting the delivery in the tutorial programme because it will support their work. The children will be supported in their learning because of the coherence this model depends on.	*Develop*. The materials are prepared and the programme for delivery is set out. Because there has been a strong focus on the needs of the children, the outcomes will be generated by the programme itself. Louise and other leaders will need to train staff to use the materials effectively, and the programme will need to be explained to the children so that they can engage fully in it.	*Operational*. At this stage the curriculum is being delivered. The staff are trained, the materials produced, the children are involved.

TABLE 3.5   (cont'd)

Task	Process	Product
5 *Experiment.* This is a new programme and so the outcomes may not match the intention – i.e. things go wrong! Louise will plan into the meetings an opportunity for the team to share their experiences. Where things are good, there is occasion for celebration. The parts which go wrong are analysed and put right.	*Refine* the model through classroom research and regular improvements.	*Refined.* The mode of operation is tailored to the desired outcomes and the needs of the team.
6 *Implement.* Having planned and delivered a programme, successes and experiences can be shared with others. The team has included core subject managers. The next stage is to develop a whole curriculum approach to study skills and to promulgate the results throughout the school.	*Change.* The curriculum has developed to embrace the needs of the children. It started by identifying good practices and needs.	A *widely used* curriculum. The programme can 'embed' itself into schemes of work and become part of the curriculum. It has been developed by a group and so will enjoy wide ownership.
7 *Evaluate the effects* of the curriculum on student learning. Louise needs to undertake some form of review with the group. She can involve the children in this review, as they were made aware of the process being developed for and with them.	*Evaluate* how effective the curriculum is.	A *proven* curriculum. The curriculum started from the needs of the children and has developed their skills. The proof lies in the obvious improvements. In the long term there will be improvements in the levels of attainment the children reach.

This process can be adapted to suit any middle manager's agenda. However, there are several points to consider when planning a strategic change.

- *Timing* – one of the characteristics of schools over the past ten years or so has been the plethora of new initiatives. It is not uncommon for teachers to denounce proposed change simply because it is change. In some organisations there is change fatigue. However, we consider that an important part of the process is ensuring that the change is realistic and needed. If teachers recognise the need for the change and the plan is a realistic one, most of them will be supportive.

- *Plan small steps and concentrate on the details* – the initiative for many of the changes going on in schools belongs to government and local authority. Whole school development issues drive other initiatives. While these may put middle managers into a reactive state, their responsibility is still to lead the change in a calm and proactive manner. By spending time planning the small steps and concentrating on the details, middle managers will demonstrate a high level of both interpersonal and organisational skill. The ability to judge exactly how long it will take to produce a set of resources will be valuable and will increase the initiative's chance of success. However, a rushed, poorly-managed project with no time for completion, or a piece of work which loses momentum, will not achieve its objectives.

- *Celebrate success and share good practice* – when the steps are completed successfully, it is important that the middle manager celebrates this with the team. A brief handwritten note will work wonders in keeping the project on track. Telling the rest of the team when a stage is completed will maintain motivation. However, if things start to go awry and a stage is in danger of missing its deadline then you will need to consider your reaction carefully. In some cases insistence on the deadline will bring out the best in those who respond well to pressure. However, this is not the time for threats! You will need to be tenacious, but in a controlled way. If the cost of achieving the long-term objective is a stage deadline then the project is worth pursuing.

- *Evaluate as you go along* – teachers will continue to work on a project if it is of benefit to the pupils they teach. However, if the objectives have to change or the materials are not working then it is important that the project manager responds accordingly. The judgement comes from deciding when to be tenacious and rigid, and when to be malleable and persuaded. These are professional judgements.

Effective project management is one of the most fulfilling aspects of middle management. It is a time when you will work closely with a small group of people (compared with the project management of a senior manager working with a much larger group). As such it is an opportunity to develop these skills. It is a time to learn about creating and managing systems. It is a time to learn about effective delegation and trust. There will be times when the project goes awry – such an occurrence needs to be regarded with a degree of pragmatism and a great deal of realism. For the most part, in schools things can be put right – they may cause inconvenience, expense and disharmony – but they can be rectified and the experience can be a profitable one.

_____ Time management _____

Classroom teachers have a good level of control over their working day. The unpredictable nature of working with people – especially children – is a factor when measuring the amount of control, but for the most part their job is to teach their classes.

However, middle managers have to both teach their own classes and manage the team. The purpose of this section is to discuss ways of coping with the wide variety of events that happen during a typical day. The important point to stress at this stage is that a middle manager's role is to _manage_ problems, not always to _solve_ problems for others. If you try to do this you will be a poorer manager as a result simply because you will have too much to do and spend your time being reactive rather than proactive.

TASK 14

Urgent versus important

1 What is important? What is urgent? Write a definition of each of these.

2 Read Table 3.6 which lists events in this head of English department's day. Categorise the events as urgent, non-urgent, important or non-important.

3 Are there any events that she could have anticipated? How should she respond to each event?

TABLE 3.6	Events in the day of the Head of English		
Event		**Urgent/important**	**Response**
1 Arrives at school to find out that a teacher is ill and has to set work for her classes.			
2 There are seven envelopes in the post for her to open.			
3 Memo from the head asking for information on last year's GCSE specification.			
4 The representative from a publishing house is calling at lunchtime to discuss requirements for the next academic year.			
5 Details of the plays being staged at the local theatre have arrived.			
6 During Lesson 2 (just before break) a boy is sent to her class saying he has been sent out from Mr Jones's class. He has no work to do and doesn't know why he has been sent out.			
7 It is her turn for break duty.			
8 There is a curriculum review meeting straight after school.			
9 There is a note from the deputy head saying that a complaint about an English teacher has been received and he needs to discuss it today.			
10 One of the English staff is working on a unit of work for Year 10 Poetry and wants some feedback on what they have produced so far.			

This would be quite a busy day and it illustrates the need to have effective strategies for managing situations as they arise. There are a number of ways in which the head of department could respond and these are discussed in Table 3.7.

TABLE 3.7   The Head of English's response

Event	Response
1 Arrives at school to find out that a teacher is ill and has to set work for her classes.	If the system for absent staff is well known, simply checking that classes are all right at the start of each lesson is sufficient. A policy where staff phone you with work might be needed. Also, it is important to have a set of 'emergency work' for such instances.
2 There are seven envelopes in the post for her to open.	Quickly scan the envelopes – any addressed to the Head of English are usually circulars and can be left for another time. Handwritten envelopes are often from parents and should receive a response during the day. If there is no money for purchasing, then there is little point in reading catalogues or circulars.
3 Memo from the head asking for information on last year's GCSE specification.	Depending on the amount of detail required, the manager can respond instantly (by return of memo) or write a holding response.
4 The representative from a publishing house is calling at lunchtime to discuss requirements for the next academic year.	Agree a time with the representative. Ensure that the representative knows what you want to discuss. It is a good idea to arrange the meeting so that it is forced to end by the bell for afternoon school.
5 Details of the plays being staged at the local theatre have arrived,	Take this home to read or pass to another person in the department whose role it is to organise such trips.
6 During Lesson 2 (just before break) a boy is sent to the class saying he has been sent out from Mr Jones's class. He has no work to do and doesn't know why he has been sent out.	Give the boy a piece of paper and tell him to write down what has happened. Carry on teaching. At a convenient point read his statement and either arrange for him to apologise or say that you will have to meet with the teacher also to sort the problem out, and that his parents will need to be informed. It is amazing how many problems resolve

TABLE 3.7 *(cont'd)*

Event	Response
	themselves! However, you will need to see Mr Jones about this incident. Department policy may need to be amended so that if children are sent out of class they have work to do.
7 It is her turn for break duty.	You have to do this and should not shirk from it.
8 There is a curriculum review meeting straight after school.	Plan for this meeting by reading the notes and doing any necessary preparation the night before.
9 There is a note from the deputy head saying that a complaint about an English teacher has been received and he needs to discuss this today.	Write to the deputy and say that you are free after the curriculum review meeting or suggest another time.
10 One of the English staff is working on a unit of work for Year 10 Poetry and wants some feedback on what they have produced so far.	When organising the work with the team arrange the deadline in advance. Ask the teacher to give you a sample of the work, with notes to explain what he has done, and say that you will review it for the next day.

The ability to manage yourself and the team is a skill which takes time to acquire and needs to be practised. However, by trying to be calm and measured in your response, the outcomes are likely to be better.

There are a number of adages which can be useful to consider when organising a day.

■ *More haste less speed* – it is important to work hard, but trying to do too many things usually results in either things going wrong or jobs not done to satisfaction.

■ *A stitch in time saves nine* – tackling small problems as they arise requires less time and effort than letting them escalate into big problems.

- *Try to handle each piece of paper once* – this is hard to do! However, if you can train yourself to respond rather than to carry memos and the like about with you, it is quite an achievement.

- *If it isn't broken, don't try to fix it* – sometimes by doing nothing a problem will resolve itself. Occasionally intervening can make a problem worse – this is the value of experience and advice.

- *It is better to lose the battle and win the war* – in the grand scheme of things, it may be better to give way over minor issues and save intransigence for the important ones.

Managing a team is challenging and those who execute their duties successfully have to learn hard lessons. The first lessons will come in the first few weeks when the transition is made from classroom teacher to middle manager. It is important to reflect on these experiences. They are there to learn from. Among the staff there will be others who have had similar experiences – it is important to find peers in whom you can trust. The need for support can be great and having those who understand the pressures will be a huge comfort. Remember too the headteacher and senior managers in the school – they are there to support your work and they will want to know what you are doing. The leadership team will have been middle managers at some time during their careers and the voice of experience can be a source of valuable counsel and encouragement.

Summary

At the end of this chapter, it is our intention that you will:

- have analysed the new post

- have considered the etiquette for leaving your current post

- have prepared for the first meeting with the headteacher

- have prepared for the first meeting with the team

- be prepared to interview and observe all the members of the team

- be able to create a team profile, using data to inform your judgements

- be able to manage the stress of the new role and manage your time efficiently

- understand the change process and be able to implement strategic change.

———— Reference ————

Gibbons, M. (1977) 'Beyond the Sabre-Toothed Curriculum', *Approaches to Curriculum Management*, Ed. Preedy, M. (1992), Milton Keynes: the Open University Press.

chapter four

Two is good but four is better

– organising meetings and the school network

Introduction

School structures are curious things – they vary considerably from one place to another. What is the accepted way of organising a school in one part of the country can appear strangely different in another. Often the structures that we see in our schools have developed over time. They may have started out with a very straightforward model but have evolved to take account of initiatives, and indeed individual school needs. The requirement, in 2006, for schools to undertake a restructuring was an attempt to give schools the scope to 'start again' and create a new structure focused on teaching and learning first and foremost. It was not meant to be an assimilation exercise but the costs of implementing a new structure (where new roles were created and old ones safeguarded for a period of three years) added up to make a difficult management situation for many schools. However, it did give schools the opportunity to rethink how they were led and managed. The emphasis was placed fairly and squarely on responsibilities that impacted on teaching and learning, with an absolute requirement to accommodate the miscellany of administrative and ancillary tasks to support staff.

However, what we started out with, and what still remains, is a school that has a headteacher, a leadership team (where one person is designated as the person who will deputise for the headteacher) and in most secondary schools staff with responsibilities for curriculum teams (the head of subject role), for groups of pupils (the head of year role) plus a range of other cross-curricular roles, whole-school roles and third-layer roles (second in department for example). How do all these fit together and how do they interface? Schools – big and small – are human organisations – we meet with other people, we are accountable to other people, we discuss with other people. In this chapter we are going to discuss how the middle manager engages with all the different groups within the school and how networking within the school and outside of the school can be managed to mutual benefit. One of the paradoxes of school life is that there is always more that can be done – managing all the demands so that you maintain your focus on what is best use of your time (and that of your team) is an important skill to develop.

In this chapter we are also going to consider what it means to be line managed and how to manage other people. People working at this level will often be part of peer groups (such as heads of department or heads of year) and we discuss how to maximise the impact that you will have. Schools have the opportunity to work as part of networked communities

– for example the *Specialist Schools and Academies Trust* has a range of networks for development and research. We discuss how to get involved in these opportunities.

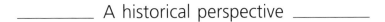 A historical perspective

Schools are characterised by their hierarchies. Perkin (1969) has suggested that in England during the nineteenth century the rapidly expanding middle classes were the 'pugnacious protagonists of the ideology of free and open competition, epitomised by examinations'. In the nineteenth century public schooling was recounted as being a life of order, regularity and serious purpose in religion, study and games (Heward, 1984). Schools were organised into finely graded hierarchies, pupils were ranked by form. Between the wars there was an increase in the central control of the many examination bodies which had grown up piecemeal in the nineteenth century. The gradual reform and introduction of statutory control in different professions since 1850 ensured that by 1930 most had minimum ages and educational qualifications for entry, and a substantial training period. Training varied from the lengthy part-time training in banking and accountancy to the five years' university education needed in medicine. In some professions, promotion also depended on further examination success. A number of professions were organised in a hierarchy of seniority, with an associated ladder of promotion for the ambitious to scale – from curate to archbishop for example. Heward (1984) describes how the bureaucratisation and professionalisation of the leading professions led to the notion of a career as a systematic preparation and training followed by regular progress to a senior position in an established and respected occupation. Attempts to impose business models on schools have, in many ways, emphasised the hierarchical structures, which are traditional and have been the cause of much difficulty. In the past, teachers were led by a headteacher or chief master or high mistress – or whatever title had been given to them. As the job became more complicated there developed the jobs of heads of subjects, deputy head teachers and the like. The introduction of promoted posts, such as year heads, deputy year heads, phase coordinators etc., is comparatively recent and underlines the complexity of the leadership and management role. However, the restructuring that schools undertook as part of the progression from management allowances to TLR (teaching and learning responsibility) payments has led to a rethink of how schools organise leadership and management to ensure that the necessary jobs get done and that people are appropriately remunerated.

In many schools, teachers have multiple roles. In most primary schools the deputy head is also a class teacher. In secondary schools, the subject head will be a class teacher and usually a pastoral tutor as well. In this context the subject head is a manager and leader to his/her team and also an integral part of the teaching team, but is also subject to the line management of a pastoral head (such as head of year, head of upper school etc.). In addition, this person is also line managed by, perhaps, a deputy head and is ultimately accountable to the headteacher. In many ways this is what makes school management complex – staff are both managers and managed, leaders and led. Taken to conclusion, class teachers are managers of learning and have that role for all their classes. This aspect of school leadership has to be borne in mind when considering the stance to take when line managing your team, and also when meeting with your own line manager.

———— Line management ————

Line management is challenging and has to be practised in order to be undertaken successfully. It requires clarity of thought and some precision. In some situations it will require tenacity and determination, and such instances will be discussed in greater detail later in this section.

Getting down to the business of managing the team needs to be thought through – as the team leader you are accountable for the outcomes of the team. In some schools this will have been stated more explicitly than in others – how much progress you are able to make in the first period of your tenure will depend to a very great extent on what systems the school has in place.

We use the term 'line management', although we accept that it is problematic. It implies that individuals are accountable to just one person and, as noted above, staff have many different roles in schools and so it's neither as simple nor straightforward as that. Also, by using the term 'management', we are of course leaving out the important aspect of leadership. Talking about 'line leadership and management' is a bit clumsy and so, therefore, we hope that the more enlightened view of the way we work with people will be apparent from the suggestions made.

At its most fundamental, leading a team is about making sure that people have clear job descriptions, that there are appropriate expectations and that lines of communication are open.

First of all, a clear and precise job description is an important element in the process. Fundamentally, people have an absolute right to know what is expected of them – they need to be involved in the construction of the job description and be aware of what they are expected to do. The process of drawing up the job description might be undertaken by the head-teacher but, equally, may be delegated to the team leader. There is a detailed discussion of how this can be effected at whole-school level in Tranter and Percival (2006).

The line manager

At its most fundamental, being a line manager involves ensuring that both parties are clear about what the other is doing, having expectations of one another and having a consistent professional dialogue that enables the job to get done and each other to benefit from the relationship. It is not about being friends. As a manager, you often have to make decisions. In some cases these will be unpopular – hopefully there will be unanimity but at least your colleagues should know why you have made the decision (if called to make it alone) and will understand your rationale. A good relationship is one in which there are no surprises, for either party.

The list in Table 4.1 is really the bedrock of an effective relationship and we will be discussing how each of these can be organised as part of the middle manager's process through the case studies.

There are a number of aspects of line management which should be in place:

- policies
- procedures
- communication
- reporting.

TABLE 4.1   Line management

- Start with a clear job description.
- Make the expectations clear.
- Establish a clear contract.
- Establish lines of communication.
- Keep accurate records.
- Celebrate success and respond to difficulties early on.

You should first ensure that there are policies which detail the remit of the team. For a subject leader or curriculum coordinator these will include policies on:

- aims of the subject
- behaviour management
- target setting
- setting and grouping
- reporting to parents
- marking and assessment
- use of ICT in the subject
- cross-curricular initiatives
- spiritual, moral, cultural and personal development
- staff development
- equal opportunities.

The importance of these policies is that they describe the work of the team and explain how these issues are to be addressed in the work of the team. In all cases, such policies should be in line with whole school policies – however, there will be subject-specific areas that require closer definition, as this case study illustrates.

CASE STUDY

Joanne – improving delivery

Joanne is maths coordinator at Laney Primary School. The recent Key Stage 2 maths results are satisfactory but have not risen in line with Joanne's predictions. Joanne has worked with all the teachers to develop a scheme of work which details the content for each unit of work, and the numeracy hour is progressing nicely. Joanne looks through all the test papers and sees that there are a number of areas of weakness in Year 6. She arranges a meeting with the headteacher to discuss her plans for the next year.

This is a familiar situation for many of those in the middle management role. There are schemes of work that detail the content of lessons and there are resources to support this work. There are a number of issues which arise in this case study – the programme of study has been set down as part of the strategy, however, the tasks for Joanne are:

- to ensure that the numeracy hour is being delivered
- to ensure that the programme of study is being followed
- to ensure that standards of attainment are raised.

Programmes of study can only take a group so far. By setting out dates, themes, content, resources etc., the middle manager can do much to improve the curriculum that is offered to children and delivered by teachers. However, in order that the programme of study is maximised there are a number of steps which need to be taken (see Table 4.2) and these will be discussed in detail.

TABLE 4.2   Stages Joanne needs to follow

Stages

1 Construct a monitoring system to support the programme of study.

2 Communicate the system to those in the team and to the line manager.

3 Develop the schemes of work through a programme.

4 Use the principle of assessment and the aims of target setting to raise standards.

———— Monitoring ————

Earlier we described the complexity of the middle management function and related this to the multiplicity of roles undertaken by you, the postholder. It is essential to develop systems which do not place an unreasonable burden on you – you still have your own classes to teach and the importance of this is clear. To be a successful middle manager, you need to be an excellent classroom practitioner.

Middle managers need to develop their professional competence to the highest standards. This is, in our view, fundamental to effective leadership. The best middle managers are also the best teachers because they are able to develop their remit with the commitment to the classroom at the fore. All systems and procedures should work to promote and facilitate the highest classroom standards. They should not detract from this. Developing strong classroom skills that promote and maximise learning is a lifelong challenge and is the core purpose of anyone teaching in a school.

Therefore, systems need to be in place to enable you to focus on the purpose of monitoring – otherwise they are onerous and occasionally futile. Monitoring, at a *functional level*, is about ensuring that the curriculum is being delivered – that things are being done. If that is all that happens (and that might be a big step in some organisations) it misses an opportunity to undertake the analysis to facilitate quality assurance – the *analytical level*.

TASK 15

Analytical and functional monitoring

This task asks you to consider these two levels of monitoring and how you, as a middle manager, might monitor the work of a team.

The table lists the activities that are undertaken by teachers at Joanne's school (from the case study on page 100). Table 4.3 shows how the monitoring can be separated into functional and analytical monitoring.

TABLE 4.3   Teacher activities at Joanne's school

Element from the programme of study	Monitoring at the functional level	Monitoring at the analytical level
1 Pupils will work through the exercises in the textbook resource.	■ Regular scrutiny of teachers' records. ■ Regular scrutiny of pupils' exercise books. ■ Monitoring of mark books. ■ Classroom observation – comparing lesson notes with expected stage.	■ Qualitative analysis of the work produced by pupils. ■ Regular discussion of pupils' progress. ■ Progress checks.
2 Pupils will conduct a survey and produce a wall display.	■ The wall display is completed. ■ The wall display is mathematically accurate.	■ Children are able to describe the processes of surveys and representation of data critically. ■ Qualitative analysis of the work produced by pupils.

TABLE 4.3 *(cont'd)*

Element from the programme of study	Monitoring at the functional level	Monitoring at the analytical level
3 Pupils will use their survey to produce graphs using Excel.	■ Produce a rota for pupils to receive teaching on Excel. ■ Pupils follow the rota and use Excel.	■ Qualitative analysis of work produced by pupils.
4 Pupils will complete unit tests on each topic.	■ Test is set and completed. ■ Questions set follow the programme of study and cover the necessary material.	■ Set targets and compare progress. ■ Receive progress reports. ■ Pupils produce subject reviews.

Functional monitoring

There are a number of ways in which monitoring at a functional level can be undertaken.

■ Produce a timetable – for example to use ICT facilities, use the sports equipment etc.

■ Incorporate the use of specialist equipment or particular units of work into the scheme of work.

■ Make the use of the equipment or the delivery of a new unit of work part of the assessment process – i.e. the assessment of pupils cannot be completed without delivering the unit of work.

■ Link units of work together.

■ Develop common systems for record keeping so that the records fall into particular categories – this will emphasise the need to complete the work.

■ Informal discussion.

■ On student reviews, ask questions that require students to comment on all the different aspects of the work.

This list is endless – the important feature of all these suggestions is that they rely on the teacher to deliver the work and not on the middle manager to engage in a long process of checking. To check that every student has done a piece of work – perhaps using Excel or Word or Access – will take a great deal of time. It is far better for middle managers to spend their time undertaking analytical monitoring. This will improve the quality of teaching and learning and be more effective in the development of the subject or curriculum area.

Analytical monitoring

Analytical monitoring is, by its very nature, more effective because it requires the teacher and middle manager to engage in some kind of dialogue based around the student's work. It has four stages.

- *Quantitative* – this may be relevant here. For example, in some areas the amount of work produced is significant. While few would argue that quantity is any kind of substitute for quality (and this is not our view) certain curriculum areas will need to make some kind of judgement. Clearly, students will not make good progress if they are not doing much work! However, there is a balance – lots of work at the same level is worse! The middle manager has to assess how the quantity of work compares with expected norms.

- *Level of work* – is the level of work appropriate? Is the work produced at the expected level? If the students are making good progress at the levels indicated by the schemes of work, the middle manager can be satisfied with the work being done. However, the middle manager may need to make an assessment and judge the levels accordingly.

- *Qualitative* – this kind of judgement varies according to the remit of the team. The middle manager can make links to target setting. The middle manager will need to assess the quality of work and the level at which each individual student is working. Qualitative monitoring is about reviewing what each student is doing – it is vital to undertake this process in the context of a full review. It does take quite a time to do because it involves considering the target levels and assessing progress against these targets. However, the resulting analysis will inform the middle manager about the progress being made by the class and will facilitate a focused discussion on the salient points.

- *Evaluative* – as part of a team review, the middle manager might evaluate the work produced and could involve the teacher in the process.

In this context, monitoring becomes a dynamic process – the teacher uses the work of the class to communicate with the middle manager. Together they discuss the work of the students and use this to set targets for the work of the individual students.

Functional or analytical?

Many middle managers will wish to undertake the analytical monitoring processes. However, if the work of the team is at a fairly early stage then functional monitoring is appropriate. You need to take a long-term view on this if you are to bring about long-lasting change which makes a difference to students' attainments. Planning the nature of monitoring as part of the development process will enable you and the team to measure progress.

There is, of course, a third way – and that is for analytical monitoring to be undertaken as a group activity. The benefit of this approach is that it is possible to secure agreement about what is expected through group discussion. The first stage is to have this as an item on the department or team meeting agenda. Some teams will benefit from having a 'blank sheet of paper' approach; others may prefer a discussion document setting out the pros and cons, listing the issues that need to be considered. Whichever approach you choose it is important to have done a lot of the thinking beforehand. Try to think through the possible objections to the approach you are proposing so that when objections are raised – they inevitably will be at some stage – you do not get deflected from the agenda by having to defer to what has been raised as problematic.

The benefit of the 'blank sheet of paper' approach is that it gives everyone the opportunity to contribute and the principles can be worked up through discussion. Having had the discussion and set down the principles for monitoring then people can assess their own work and that of others, using the agreed process. This is consultative management and is an excellent way of raising standards through a shared understanding.

However, things do go wrong and it is likely that at some point a member of the team will be found wanting and the outcomes from the monitoring process will tell you about the team's capability. You need to handle such data with sensitivity but also a measure of detachment. It is important that you learn to separate collegial loyalty from the demands of your role and the responsibility you have. This is not an easy transition to make as Task 16 illustrates.

Results of monitoring

As Numeracy Coordinator Joanne has set up a system for monitoring the numeracy hour delivery.

She arranges to sample the books from all classes to review the progress being made on the plans to improve the teaching of shape. She samples five books from each class.

The unit of work the Year 6 teacher prepared on 'patterns in polygons' has been done in a very cursory manner. The work produced by the children is poorly done and there are some incorrect references.

The other topics have been done to a satisfactory standard.

Joanne is line manager to the Year 6 teacher. What actions should she take?

This scenario is not uncommon for middle managers because it illustrates the integral nature of school management systems. School management depends heavily on cooperation simply because teachers have a high level of autonomy in their classrooms, and this is emphasised by the isolated nature of the teaching task.

There are at least four questions that Joanne will need to ask.

- *How was the unit of work created?* Teachers in middle management roles often create units of work for pupils to do to address certain issues and to meet specific objectives. However, ways need to be found to engage all the users in this creative process. Possibilities include sharing pieces of work as they are created and dividing up the unit of work so that all the users will contribute to the whole piece. Otherwise, the opportunity to review the unit of work needs to be made during a meeting time – putting such an item on an agenda creates a climate for sharing and collaboration. It also means that objections and difficulties can be managed appropriately. Successful implementation of measures depends not only on the quality of work undertaken, but also on the strategies Joanne uses to introduce her solution. In addition, any training necessitated by a new initiative needs to be built into the lead-time before a project comes on line.

- *What are the assessment objectives and do they match the required outcomes?* In any curriculum plan, the assessment needs to be integrated into the tasks. To do otherwise is to create a monster – the curriculum is sufficiently full in itself. The range of assessment opportunities has to be mapped out across the curriculum otherwise it is piecemeal and lacks coherence. The assessment objectives should be made clear at the start of the unit of work – this has the effect of raising the profile of the assessment process. If ways can be found to incorporate pupil or student assessment into the task then so much the better. For example, a unit of work in a foreign language might have the following objectives.

By the end of the unit of work on drinks, the student will:

- know the words in French for a range of beverages
- be able to spell the words accurately
- have participated in role-plays to purchase a drink in a café
- have written a conversation between a café owner and a person ordering drinks.

Such objectives might be assessed using tests, oral assessment and assessment of written work. However, by informing pupils of the assessment objectives they could assess their own progress at the end of the time period. By linking teaching, pupil assessment and teacher assessment together – perhaps in some kind of grid in a pupil's folder – the need for the teacher to undertake his/her tasks is emphasised. Few teachers can ignore the pupils who insist on the work being done to fulfil their learning objectives (and enable them to fill in their grids)!

- *Does the teacher have sufficient knowledge to deliver the unit of work?* This is where the work becomes difficult. A sensitive middle manager will know the profile of the team and anticipate the training needs of the teachers. However, the reluctance which an experienced teacher (particularly one in a promoted post) will demonstrate cannot be underestimated. There are teachers who, like many other people, will become adept at disguising their lack of knowledge. Joanne can approach this issue by providing guidance which spells out the knowledge required. Joanne might discuss the matter with the teacher – it may be appropriate for her and the teacher to plan and rehearse the lesson, or she might deliver a sample lesson as part of a training session, or arrange for the teacher to observe her delivering the unit of work. However she tackles this issue, the responsibility for addressing the problem is hers – the pupils need to be taught by a person secure in their knowledge of the subject. It is incumbent on Joanne to ensure that this is the case, and to make appropriate arrangements otherwise.

■ *What is the problem?* The problem may have been a local issue – there may have been circumstances about which Joanne is unaware which prevented the class teacher from delivering the unit of work at the specified time. This needs to be discussed openly and Joanne and the teacher should then agree on a programme to address any deficiencies caused by this lapse in standards. At this stage, having agreed a programme, Joanne has to make it clear how she will monitor the remedial work – it might be appropriate for her to see all of the books from the class to ensure the tasks are complete.

It is possible that, in the course of such a discussion, a wide range of issues might emerge. These can range from issues to do with personal organisation to disaffection to obstinacy. Joanne needs to anticipate these possible reactions and respond accordingly. However, her response will be easier if there has been transparency and clarity of purpose – subterfuge and manipulation are rarely successful in the long term. It is our view that it is always good advice to act with integrity and honesty. There may be difficulties, but manipulating people or the facts does not ease these – they certainly do not engender respect. Taking on colleagues is never easy. However, the ability to 'move teachers on' – whether this means from incompetence to dismissal, poor performance to satisfactory performance, or very good to excellence – is the hallmark of a highly effective middle manager.

Table 4.4 summarises features of the monitoring process which need to be considered.

TABLE 4.4   Characteristics of effective monitoring

Effective and efficient monitoring is characterised by:

■ thinking about monitoring as work is planned

■ agreeing as a team on the monitoring process

■ careful analysis of the needs of the students

■ planning to address student needs

■ using assessment opportunities to inform planning

TABLE 4.4 *(cont'd)*

- integrating assessment processes into the teaching programme

- exploring opportunities for student self-assessment

- using the creative stages of units of work as a development tool

- making the monitoring aspect explicit to students and their teachers

- carrying out the monitoring as planned in an equitable manner and responding to issues as they arise

- keeping records of the stages in the process and the outcomes.

———— Being managed ————

The previous section dealt with how to approach the line management of staff to ensure that the functional aspects of the job are delivered appropriately. The middle manager is not the end of the line, however. You are responsible to your own line manager, who might be the deputy head or the headteacher depending on the size of the school and the nature of the role. The way in which you approach your own responsibilities for accountability is an important aspect of your work.

The situational aspect of the job is clearly fundamental to this debate. In a small school where there are close working relationships, conversations will be dominant and there is scope for regular reports to the line manager. In a large school however, interactions with your line manager may be infrequent. One can envisage in a split-site school a face-to-face conversation occurring perhaps weekly at best. Whatever the situation there are a number of considerations for the middle manager.

In the early stages of a relationship there is considerable value in the middle manager advising the line manager of all activity (the 'need to know'). This will give the line manager confidence in the middle manager's ability to discharge duties efficiently and effectively. As time goes on the middle manager's confidence grows and with it the line manager's confidence in the middle manager, so there will be less need to inform about everything.

There are some items of information which we would suggest are relayed as a minimum:

- meeting agendas
- minutes of meetings
- development plans

- job descriptions
- letters to parents and to other agencies
- memoranda to the whole team
- budget statements
- issues which might be the precursor to disciplinary procedures.

Being line-managed is about ensuring that your line manager is clear about the work that you are doing. By keeping your line manager supplied with information and progress reports, they can support you in what you do (see Table 4.5).

TABLE 4.5 Being line-managed

- Copy-in your line manager when you write memoranda.
- Discuss potential difficulties – particularly those concerning performance review and performance management.
- Discuss planning development activities with your line manager to gain support.
- Use your line manager as a 'critical friend' when planning new ideas and controversial initiatives.
- Keep accurate records of the meetings you have.

Performance review

The subject of performance review has been a source of political and professional difficulty for many years – a more detailed discussion of the issues is given in Tranter and Percival (2006).

Effective performance review must be embedded into the professional management of staff. To limit any performance review system to an assessment of the teacher's performance in the classroom is to neglect the wider role that many teachers have – particularly in the case of middle managers. The legislated purpose of performance review is to assist school teachers in their professional development, and career planning and decision makers in their management of school teachers to promote the quality of education through assisting teachers to realise their potential and carry out their duties more effectively.

It is important to state, at this early stage, that performance review may not be used as a disciplinary sanction. Gold and Szemerenyi (1997)

TABLE 4.6   Gold and Szemerenyi's appraisal system objectives

- To recognise the achievements of teachers and help identify ways of improving their skills and performance.

- To assist teachers, the governing body and (where relevant) the local authority in determining whether a change of duties would help professional development and career prospects.

- To identify potential for career development supported by in-service training.

- To assist teachers who are experiencing difficulties by offering guidance, training and counselling.

- To inform those responsible for providing references.

- To improve the management of schools.

set out the objectives that any performance review system should represent. These are given in Table 4.6.

Many middle managers will be subject to processes that have been drawn up at whole-school level, but there are a number of issues that need to be considered by someone like you who will be implementing a system.

- What is the function of performance review?
- What information is required?
- How should data be collected?
- How should the process be managed?
- How should difficult issues be tackled?
- How can targets be set to facilitate professional development?
- What do I do if it goes wrong?

The next part of this section deals with each of these issues in turn.

What is the function of performance review?

The principle of performance review is that it should be a summative statement of a teacher's performance as a professional. It should not, therefore, be restricted to a set of statements about the teacher's classroom performance – for middle managers, in particular, there are potential dangers in this narrow perspective. Although we would argue that the most important role for middle managers is excellence in the classroom, the function of middle managers is far wider than that.

It is important that middle managers are excellent classroom practitioners. Their role is to guide their team towards improved classroom skill and the middle manager needs to be able to demonstrate those practices personally. In some ways, this illustrates the complex nature of middle management in schools – of which much has been said already – that the middle manager is the leader and manager of a team, but also has a full teaching load. It is difficult to avoid cliches when describing this state, but being able to 'hack it' in the classroom is of fundamental importance in establishing and maintaining credibility in the school in general and the team in particular. This is why you need to ensure that the standards you set are practised in your own classroom – to do otherwise leaves you open to challenge at best, to ridicule at worst.

Therefore, we suggest that the performance review process should encompass all aspects of the teacher's work and, for the middle manager, reflect the role the middle manager has. There are many ways in which this can be managed and local agreement and pro formas may specify the procedures. However, there is scope for the middle manager to define the parameters of the performance review process but this needs to be debated with the leadership team in the school.

A good place to start, however, is with the job description. This statement is contractual and it provides a basis against which the teacher's performance can be assessed. A good job description includes not only the task of teaching classes, but also those additional responsibilities which the teacher has as part of his/her remit. Thus, by looking at the performance of the teacher against these specifications, the performance reviewer has a sound and non-contentious basis on which to begin.

One way of managing this is to develop a performance review preparation process. The language is complicated here and so we are using the terms 'appraiser' and 'appraisee' to signify the two roles. This process has distinct stages. The appraiser gives the appraisee a copy of the job description. Both parties assess the appraisee's performance as:

- *successful* – with supporting evidence

- *needing development* – a competence which is in need of development or

- *unsure* – when it cannot be stated with clarity or there is insufficient evidence to support either view.

By assessing each of the areas in terms of a competence rating, the agenda for the performance review process becomes clear. Where there is agreement on the areas and both parties agree that the work is successful, there is the opportunity for praise and the performance review has already achieved a positive outcome. Where both parties rate performance as needing development, there can be an assessment of the progress already made and a programme of support can be agreed. Where either party is unsure the matter can be debated or evidence cited to support the perception.

Where parties disagree the issue needs to be discussed, but the primary outcome of this first stage is that the focus for the performance review is clear. If there is disagreement, the appraiser and appraisee need to be able to cite evidence to plead a case. There has to be a caveat in all performance management systems that where there is major irreconcilable disagreement, the assertion of the appraiser forms the performance review statement, but that the appraisee has the right to record disagreement and that this note is included in the record.

However, this matter does raise an important question regarding the function of the performance review process. It should not, in our view, be a mechanistic process where the two parties wait to tell one another what they think – to this end, the process should be summative. If the performance review process is used for the middle manager to express disquiet about the teacher's work then it is an abuse of the process. Similarly if the procedure is the only time when a teacher's work is recognised positively, it is poor management. An effective performance review should not produce surprises, it should be an honest summative statement which details the teacher's successes and performance as measured against the criteria set down. It needs to be formative because without outcomes it lacks any kind of 'teeth' and can become a cosy nebulous chat with little to benefit either party.

Collecting data

A variety of information can be used to carry out a performance assessment of a teacher. However, in order to make the process fair and open, you should consider what type of information you are going to collect.

TASK 17

Collecting information for a performance review

There are different types of information and data that will be required for a performance review interview. Some of these will be qualitative or quantitative, others factual and some attitudinal.

The *Threshold Standards* are a useful benchmark in considering the domains of evidence (see www.teachernet.gov.uk/performancethreshold for the full text).

To analyse your own performance, find evidence of your work against each of the standards. Having done this, assess what skills and experience you need in order to improve. Preparing to do a review of a colleague requires you to go through this process with them.

1 Knowledge and understanding

Have a thorough and up-to-date knowledge of the teaching of their subject(s) and take account of wider curriculum developments which are relevant to their work. This is a difficult one to quantify but a person's INSET record is relevant, as is the extent to which the teacher keeps up to date with new developments – in this task, a teacher who did not incorporate ICT into their teaching because they did not know how to use the software would need to improve their knowledge and understanding.

2.1 Teaching and assessment – planning lessons

Consistently and effectively plan lessons and sequences of lessons to meet pupils' individual learning needs. The programme of study that forms the bedrock of the team's collaborative planning is part of the evidence base, if the teacher has contributed to its development or review. However, a programme of study is a general document which the individual teacher personalises to accommodate the needs of the pupils in the class. Evidence of tailoring the programme to the class is the evidence base for this area of performance appraisal.

2.2 Teaching and assessment – classroom management

Consistently and effectively use a range of appropriate strategies for teaching and classroom management. In this section appropriate domains of evidence would be the records of lesson observations and the extent to which the individual is successful at managing classes.

2.3 Teaching and assessment – monitoring progress

Consistently and effectively use information about prior attainment to set well-grounded expectations for pupils and monitor progress to give clear and constructive feedback. Again, the records that a teacher keeps to monitor the progress of the pupils in the classes is the appropriate domain of evidence. Of course, this is not only about academic progress but evidence of planning and progress for children with special educational needs and *Every Child Matters* is appropriate to include.

3 Pupil progress

Pupils achieve well relative to the pupils' prior attainment, making progress as good as or better than similar pupils nationally. The department's target-setting policy is an important point of reference as the progress that individuals and groups make can be easily referenced to the marks or grades in any relevant national tests or examinations, or school-based assessment for pupils where national tests and examinations are not taken.

4.1 Wider professional effectiveness – personal development

Teachers are required to take responsibility for their professional development and use the outcomes to improve their teaching and pupils' learning. The individual INSET record is a good source of evidence but while external courses are one way of getting training, the five school-based INSET days are another. Indeed, if you take an enlightened view of project development and involvement in working groups and the like, many activities can be considered under the heading of personal development.

4.2 Wider professional effectiveness – school development

Teachers are required to make an active contribution to school development and when they assert that they make an active contribution to the policies and aspirations of the school, then involvement in working groups and contributing to discussion at formal meetings is appropriate evidence of this. Other things to consider here are relationships with students, with parents and with other colleagues across the school.

5 Professional characteristics

Are effective professionals who challenge and support all pupils to do their best.

This data collection and analysis is necessary because it helps to clarify what you are trying to do when you are collecting data for the performance review interview. It is easy to set down a brief for the data collection which is too wide-ranging and too vague. By concentrating on the specific issues which arise from the initial performance review interview, the need for information becomes clear.

You should consider how you intend to collect the data that you need. Different ways of doing this are listed below, together with some guidance on how it can be used.

- *Quantitative data* – this type of data is needed when measuring the performance of the teacher against specific targets – for example the teacher's ability to add value to the cognitive ability targets set by the school. To do this you would need to have a list of some of the targets (e.g. the Key Stage 3 targets for the class) and compare these with the actual results. In this way you can create useful data on which to carry out the performance review process. Other examples might be the number of homework tasks set and assessed, recruitment to courses for which the teacher has particular responsibility etc.

- *Qualitative data* – this type of data is very important when considering the quality of the relationships within the team. For example, you and the teacher may choose to carry out some kind of attitudinal survey among the students to assess their attitude to the subject, the confidence they have in their teacher etc. Such a survey is not to be undertaken lightly; but if this process is managed sensitively it can produce useful information which both parties can consider in depth.

- *Teacher outputs* – a good deal of valuable information can be gleaned from examining the outputs from the teacher's work. For example, the examination of the worksheets produced will give a valuable insight into the level of work set, the standard of presentation, the amount of work set etc. This kind of data is useful when considered with attitudinal survey results and the effectiveness of the teaching assessment.

- *Classroom observation of teaching practice* – this aspect of the teacher's work is the most important for all the obvious reasons. Without effective teaching, the pupils will not be learning and the teacher is failing. The monitoring process will be used to measure the performance of teachers throughout the year, but the performance review process is useful in defining the state of a classroom teacher's work at the given time. The performance review can be of particular use here, but it should not be seen as an opportunity to tell the teacher facts about his/her teaching that have been evident throughout the year – it is unfair to use a performance review as an excuse for this.

Tackling difficult issues

Tackling difficult issues that arise from the performance review process is, in some ways, no different from the approach that should be taken at any other time. However, the increasing importance of performance review and performance management in relation to pay and advancement means that you have to be certain that your procedures are fair and that you can substantiate your judgements with evidence.

In the previous section, we discussed the need to acquire quality data in an open manner. By agreeing the type of evidence that you will collect and the means by which you will do so, you are giving the teacher the opportunity to register any disquiet with the proposals. If the teacher disputes the necessity of the data collection you have three choices.

- *To continue to negotiate with the teacher until agreement has been reached*. This clearly has a number of advantages – not least the teacher is able to see that you take the objections seriously. However, you need to prepare the case thoroughly and be confident in your assertion of the performance review process. Put simply, a disagreement at the initial stage is resolved most effectively by both parties agreeing to disagree, but both being required to produce evidence to support their case.

- *To seek clarification with your line manager*. This can be particularly useful if you are not used to carrying out performance reviews. Indeed, anyone new to this aspect of the middle management role should take advice from the management team in the school. It is important to be fully conversant with the procedures and aware of the implications and potential outcomes of your actions. The performance review process is not a disciplinary process and there must be no ambiguity about your role at this stage. When preparing to do a performance review, you should raise potential difficulties with a senior manager and discuss the actions and outcomes in detail. This will help in being secure in the steps you take when managing the performance review process.

- *Asserting your view and judgement*. As the line manager, you are empowered to state your professional judgement as the person responsible for the work of the team. However, performance review is intended to be a collaborative process and the appraisee has access to, and the right to comment on, what the appraiser says. At this juncture, the process is confined to the professional ambit of the school and so the support of the headteacher is crucial when faced with difficult situations.

An important issue at this stage in the consideration of difficult issues is what happens when the performance review process raises issues of professional competence. There are specified compulsory elements of teacher performance review and these include:

- classroom observation
- a performance review interview which will include setting targets
- preparation of a performance review statement summarising the discussion at that formal review meeting.

However, classroom observation may indicate, for example, that a teacher has difficulty in controlling classes. The correct outcome for this in the performance review context is training and guidance from more experienced colleagues. The question of target setting is discussed in the following section.

Setting targets

A fundamental element of teacher performance review is the setting of targets. To give the process some coherence, we advise setting targets in a direct response to the data collection. It is important to prepare thoroughly for this aspect of the task because, in many cases, those who need the targets will be reluctant to accept the necessity of the process at all.

In Table 4.7, we detail several outcomes from the data collection phase and suggest targets for the teacher. A target must be both measurable

TABLE 4.7   Outcomes and targets

Outcome	Target and action
Disciplinary issues raised from classroom observation	■ Training and guidance from colleagues. ■ Arrangements for the teacher to observe other staff, with specific criteria for the observation. ■ Arrangements set out to support the teacher. ■ Discussion of strategies for dealing with disciplinary matters. *Target – to improve behaviour management in class (this may be related to particular year groups, ability ranges etc.).*
Quality of teaching – pace in lessons	■ Discussion of strategies for setting and maintaining pace. ■ Lesson observation. ■ INSET on lesson planning. ■ External courses on target setting etc. *Target – to increase the quantity and quality of work done by students in class.*

TABLE 4.7 (cont'd)

Outcome	Target and action
Quality of teaching – subject knowledge	■ Identify which areas of the subject are problematic. ■ Purchase of texts to support the teacher in acquiring knowledge. ■ Discussion with a subject adviser or expert. ■ Discussion of lesson notes on particular topics. ■ Demonstration lessons given by the middle manager. *Target – to improve the subject knowledge of, for example, the Restoration/A level inorganic chemistry/use of logo etc.*
Contribution to the team effort	■ Discussion of the role of teacher as part of a team. ■ Establishing projects in which the teacher works with a variety of staff, with close monitoring. ■ Monitoring of, for example, the work produced by the teacher, against the team standard. *Target – to produce a unit of work with detailed lesson notes and resources for use by the team.*
Procedural issues	■ Clear direction by the middle manager on what needs to be done. ■ Defined reporting lines. ■ Discussion of practical issues, such as classroom layout etc. *Target – depends on the procedural issue.*
Relationships with students	■ Behaviour management courses. ■ The teacher might lead a team project on some aspect of this issue. ■ Improve the comments written on work and on reports (specify the type of comments that are desirable). *Target – that all reports should contain a summative statement and a positive outcome based on the formative assessment.*

over time and achievable. Furthermore, the actions should support the teacher and facilitate the achievement of the target – the actions should not run counter to the targets set by the appraiser.

One issue that does arise from performance review is whether a teacher is competent or not. This question should not arise from the performance review process itself; it should arise from normal monitoring. However, failure to meet acceptable standards may be a disciplinary matter to be dealt with under the laid-down procedures. You would need to report to your line manager on such matters. If the performance review process goes wrong you need to take advice on how to proceed. Table 4.8 summarises the performance review process.

Keeping in touch with colleagues is a fundamental task, and one that has to be practised assiduously to maintain high professional standards. Having regular discussions and meetings where you consider together the way in which a particular issue is being tackled and where you regularly review progress and standards will enable you to enjoy a more collaborative and productive working relationship. It makes it easier to say the

TABLE 4.8 Summary of the performance review process

- Use the teacher's job description as the starting point for the review.
- Decide on the focus for the performance review.
- Arrange and undertake classroom observation.
- Collect other data as required.
- Prepare material for the performance review interview.
- Anticipate any difficulties and discuss them with your line manager.
- Conduct the performance review interview and write a statement.
- If the appraisee does not agree with the statement, discuss the issues. If they cannot be resolved, the appraisee has the right to include a personal statement.
- Set targets for the following cycle and agree on the support and desired outcomes.
- Communicate the outcomes to your line manager.
- Monitor the progress of the teacher.
- Where discussion takes place in relation to the targets, take notes and provide the appraisee with a copy.

difficult things if there is regular dialogue – if the only time you speak to a person is when you have to give them feedback on poor performance then the relationship will never be healthy.

Managing people is one aspect of the role of middle manager – managing resources is another. Whatever difficulties may be anticipated when managing people are thrown into relief when considering those that can follow from mismanaging money and resources.

_____ Administrative control _____

Managing people is one of the major tasks of being a middle manager. It is important to make sure that the school achieves value for money for the capitation devolved to the team. The middle manager therefore needs to establish procedures for managing stock and the budget. The principle is of 'value for money' for the spending that is undertaken and absolute probity when dealing with cash.

Large sums of money are spent on textbooks and stationery in schools and in a large department it makes sense to try to secure best value for money as virement (where money allocated for one purpose can be spent on another) is often possible. Many schools which employ a bursar or business manager have protocols for securing best value – so the effort of finding the cheapest supplier will be done for you. Stock control is critical, especially in a large department where each pupil has at least one textbook – with many texts costing at least £10, losing books is an expensive way to mismanage a department. There are a number of levels of administrative control that are set out in Table 4.9.

A significant aspect of the middle manager's role will be budget responsibility. This may, in the case of a large school, be several thousands

TABLE 4.9 Administrative control

- Set out procedures for ordering books, inspection copies, equipment etc.
- Set out a way of recording issue of books to staff and students – a database is a possibility.
- Keep records of money spent on orders.
- Keep records for petty cash – negotiate accounting procedures with school administration personnel.
- Ensure that the records kept are full, documented and transparent.

of pounds to cover the needs of a large number of children. The extent to which funds are delegated to middle managers will depend on the structures in the school. Some schools have delegated funds to middle managers to include:

- purchase of stationery
- purchase of textbooks
- purchase of furniture
- INSET provision.

There are a number of computer packages which will keep account of the budget. They allow users to specify fields – for example date, supplier, order items and the status of the order. Whether you choose to use such a package or keep manual records you need to consider a number of aspects of financial management.

Record keeping

At this level there is a need to keep an accurate record of items ordered and received. Most schools will have a designated person to arrange for payment. However, we advise you to keep a log of orders and money spent so that you can easily account for the money you have been allocated.

Most teams will have a sum of money delegated to them (often called capitation). To avoid any difficulty, it is important to plan the expenditure over the year. Certainly you should prioritise expenditure and keep track of the team budget. This is good practice.

The matter of petty cash is important to raise here. Schools each have their own policies on petty cash and charging students for lost books etc. It is vital that there is transparency in all financial matters. Some kind of cashbook in which income received and paid out is advisable.

Authority for spending

Schools are visited regularly by publishing companies and teachers will receive offers about books and equipment. Publishers commonly offer inspection copies which the school can either purchase or return. You should clarify with your team the extent to which they can do this without authority. Schools with good control systems will only authorise expenditure from a budget with the agreement of the manager. However, it is worthwhile clarifying this with the leadership team and with the teachers in the team to avoid any difficulty.

Stock control

This is a difficult area for many middle managers. It is relatively easy to manage the stock if each teacher has control over their books and equipment – for example, if the books never leave the room. However, there is usually some slippage where items do go missing or are unaccounted for. The challenge is to minimise the effect of this. By issuing books to students and giving them the responsibility for the maintenance and safe-keeping of the book, there is redress if things go awry.

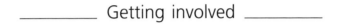

Getting involved

There may be times, perhaps, when you first begin work as a middle manager that you can barely imagine having the time or space to get involved in local or national projects! The time will come, however, when you feel able to participate. There are plenty of opportunities and one of the best is through the Specialist Schools and Academies Trust (SSAT).

Figure 4.1 shows the range of different opportunities that the trust offers.

The benefit of being involved in this type of work is that it gives you access to a wide range of practice in schools nationwide – and indeed via iNET (International Network for Education Transformation) to all over the world. SSAT provides a range of programmes and events that will enable you to find out about best practice in your subject in particular, and in teaching and learning in general. SSAT offers a range of programmes and research bursaries so that if you have an idea you may be able to secure some external funding to try it out.

Getting involved with external networks is very good personal professional development – it gives you the opportunity to test out your ideas, discuss them with others and, if appropriate, present your findings at meetings and conferences.

Many local authorities also organise network meetings for subjects and other current areas (for example assessment for learning, e-learning, work-related learning) where groups are formed as loose structures to address a shared need. Getting involved in these is equally valuable – a well-earned local reputation will pay dividends for future promotions as well as enhancing your own school's standing.

The National College for School Leadership published a leaflet in 2005 called *Networks: The potential for teacher learning* (publication code P-NETW-0905) which set out the benefits of being involved in a network and gives

FIG. 4.1 Example of Specialist Schools and Academies Trust webpage

examples of where successful collaborations based on networks have been beneficial in bringing groups of teachers together. The website www.gtce.org.uk/NetworksForTeacherLearning provides a useful introduction to the benefits.

———————— Summary ————————

At the end of this chapter, it is our intention that you will:

■ considered the nature of management in schools

■ understood the concept of line management

■ realised the importance of policies and the features of effective communication

■ considered how to monitor the work of a team

■ appreciated the need for performance review and performance management

■ considered how to link with peers and other schools.

Getting line management relationships right is critical to the progress that you are able to make as a team. There will be occasions when things go wrong – there may be 'fallings out' and disputes but sticking to the principles of good organisation and high professional standards will help you out of many a fix. It is good fun, and most of your colleagues will want to be part of the running of the team – they will want to have a say in what happens. Providing them with the means to do that through the way in which you lead the team will do much to transform a group of individuals into a high-performing team.

———————— References ————————

Gold, R. and Szemerenyi, S. (1997) *Running a School 1988: Legal Duties and Responsibilities*, Bristol: Jordans.

Heward, C. (1984) 'Parents, Sons and their Careers: A Case Study of a Public School 1930–50,' *British Public Schools: Policy and Practice*, Ed. Walford, G. (1984), London: Falmer Press.

NCSL (2005) *Networks: The potential for teacher learning* (publication code P-NETW-0905).

Perkin, H. (1969) *The Origins of Modern English Society 1780–1880*, London: Routledge and Kegan Paul.

Tranter, S. and Percival, A. (2006) *Performance Management in Schools*, London: Pearson.

Spending £100K

– recruiting new staff and monitoring performance

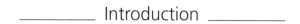

Introduction

The most important resource in a school is the staff – they can literally make or break the school. Recruitment is one of the most important tasks that we do. Get it right and a team can be transformed, get it wrong and the effects can be devastating, not only in terms of children's progress but on staff morale. Recruiting a teacher who might stay for five years is deciding how to spend at least £100,000 – an important decision that needs planning, managing and consideration.

An overview of the recruitment process

The purpose of recruitment is to make sure that you get the right person to work as part of your team. What the 'right' person looks like is difficult to describe initially and therefore undertaking some form of audit and then thinking carefully about the recruitment process is the first step.

Most of the opportunities to recruit teachers happen when someone leaves. Therefore, when a colleague tells you that they are going for an interview it is a good idea to give some thought to recruitment then.

Teachers are required to give notice before they leave, and this is two or three months (depending on the time of year) before the end of the term. Someone who intends to leave at Christmas (i.e. whose resignation date is 31 December) has to resign at the latest by 31 October. If the teacher intends to leave at the end of the academic year (i.e. 31 August) then the latest resignation date is 31 May.

The recruitment process for teachers is unwieldy because of these notice periods and, when advertising is factored into the system, it takes a long time. Working back from when a teacher might start working, an example of the process looks like Table 5.1.

This process has been compacted quite considerably as it allows just two weeks from the advertisement to the closing date, and assumes that there is a shortlisting meeting on the same day as applications close. Sending out for references happens at the same time and invitations to interview are just a week before the selection process. Because of the position of the October half term on this model, the interview is on the Friday of half term and so is at the very latest that it can happen. As you can see, moving it any earlier during the week means that the process gets pushed further and further into September.

TABLE 5.1 Recruitment timetable

Teacher resigns	Date
Advertisement placed with the TES – Monday 12 noon deadline	19 September
Advertisement appears in TES	23 September
Closing date for applications	7 October
Shortlisting and reference requests	7 October
Invitations sent out for interview	14 October
Interview	21 October (half term)
Teacher resigns from current post	31 October
Teacher starts work	Start of spring term

In many cases the recruitment timetable is forced by circumstances but if you are to have a serving teacher in post by the start of term then this schedule illustrates the need to be prepared.

Before a person starts work in a school there are some checks that need to be made:

- qualifications – does the candidate hold the qualifications that they claim?
- criminal records – the CRB check
- health questionnaire.

Some schools make additional checks – but in some cases, such as moving from one school to another school within a local authority, this process can be shortened. The school should have systems in place to ensure that these checks are undertaken.

The important point to note is that the time interval for recruitment is often very short and therefore it is beneficial to the selection team if many of the issues have been considered previously. So when a person leaves then much of the material is ready to go, leaving you the space to consider the interview and selection process more fully.

_____ How to do a staff audit _____

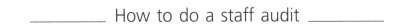

When a member of staff leaves it should be seen as an opportunity to look at the team critically and to think about what is needed for the future. It is very easy to jump straight into a replacement exercise and, although it might satisfy the immediate demand of a having a teacher in front of a class (which is very important!), it might end up with the school missing out on the chance to add a new dimension to its staff portfolio.

The decision to recruit a teacher to the team may be taken in the light of a resignation, a retirement or even increasing curriculum responsibility which necessitates the enlargement of the team.

Whatever the reason, there needs to be a review of the state of the team to assess its needs and to consider how it may change over the next few years. The purpose of this is to ensure that the recruitment process results in the appointment of a teacher whose skills and attributes match most closely the needs of the team.

There are several questions to consider when conducting such an audit. Table 5.2 provides a template for such a process, with accompanying notes.

At the end of this audit process you will have a clear view of what kind of teacher needs to be appointed to the team. The appointment process does not, of course, take place in a vacuum. There is the need for any appointment to fit in with the needs of the school as a whole – the school may be looking for opportunities to increase the numbers of staff who can coach particular sports, or contribute to the extracurricular life of the

TABLE 5.2 Team needs audit pro forma

Factor	Notes and questions
Age profile of the team	■ What is the age profile of the team? ■ What is the mean age? ■ Is the subject area seen as a 'young' subject? ■ Are there particular advances in the subject which make this an issue?
Subject expertise of the team	■ Is the team well placed for curriculum development? ■ Is there an aspect of the team's work that needs greater subject expertise – for example, is there a need for the teacher to be a scientist, so that they can act as science coordinator.
Length of service in the school	■ Clearly when recruiting from outside the school, this is less of an issue – however, the overall profile of teaching experience is relevant.

TABLE 5.2 (cont'd)

Factor	Notes and questions
Teaching expertise in the team	■ Are there areas of teaching skill that need to be addressed? For example, is there a lack of skill in teaching particular aspects of the curriculum, such as delivering ICT?
Team development plan	■ How will the departure of a teacher (from the existing team) affect the plans for the future? ■ Is there a specific responsibility which needs to be undertaken?
Developments in the team's remit	■ There may be new tasks which will come 'on line' in the near future. Is this an opportunity to appoint a person who can take these on?
Succession planning opportunities	■ By considering the profile of the team as it stands, there may be opportunities to reshape the team and provide the scope for further development.

school. You do not have to be parochial but you do have to decide what is required for the work of the team.

Of course any recruitment process will require some form of compromise – it is unlikely that you will be able to recruit Superman who will be able to do all of the things you will want as well as be a brilliant teacher, but having some idea of what skills will enhance the team development is a good outcome from the audit process.

In this discussion we have only considered recruiting a teacher – many schools allocate support staff to departments and teams, such as a technician, administrator or teaching assistant. Going through the same process, thinking about what skills you would ideally like to enhance the team's performance is critical to successful recruitment.

Drawing up job descriptions and person specifications

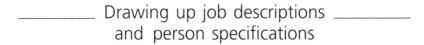

This part of the process might already be part of the school's systems – some schools have generic job descriptions that apply to all people who hold particular positions of responsibility. However, it is worth asking if you can personalise the job description to the needs of your team. Certainly under the restructuring exercise carried out in 2005/06 for TLR payments then the role should have a job description and be part of the staffing structure in the school.

The job description

The job description should set out what you want the person to do and, as such, it is a really important document to get right – it is how you are going to sell the job to prospective colleagues.

The job description should not be just a list of things that you expect the person to do. A good job description should set down the areas of responsibility and the expected outcomes. This is an important distinction but one that needs to be incorporated into the process as it means that the successful candidate will be able to see this role as part of their own career development. Thinking about this from the candidate's point of view will help to recruit high calibre personnel.

The job description should focus the person's work on teaching and learning rather than administrative tasks. This sounds obvious but when you start from the 'blank piece of paper' it is easier to come up with a list of jobs (perhaps the ones you dislike) rather than thinking about giving responsibility for specific areas of the team's work.

CASE STUDY

An opportunity

Lauren is head of modern foreign languages at Begley School. The school currently teaches Italian and Russian but there have been difficulties recruiting suitably qualified Russian teachers and results have been weakening over the recent period. Lauren wants to introduce French into the curriculum and she knows that there is sufficient mastery of Russian among the current staff to fulfil the requirements whilst it is phased out. When the team undertook its last self-evaluation it revealed weaknesses in oracy. One of the Russian teachers is retiring and Lauren has to draw up a recruitment pack for a replacement teacher.

This is a really good opportunity for the department. The curriculum review supports the head of department's view that the second language needs to change and there is a recruitment opportunity as well.

What needs to happen is that the job description has to be drawn up so that a person is recruited who is capable of teaching French and Italian (the actual weight of these can be determined by an analysis of the staff proficiency) and there is also an opportunity to create a role that specifically addresses oracy in the department. This is the difference between giving people a list of jobs to do and providing them with responsibility and career development.

Instead of drawing up a job description that lists – organising set lists, organising oral exams for GCSE, writing schemes of work to promote speaking in the target language, producing exam papers for lower school French – a good job description will express a way of establishing what the outcomes will be of the tasks, and phrasing the role accordingly.

Taking two of the tasks in the previous paragraph:

1 *Organising set lists* – this is a very important job because it's about ensuring that children are in the most appropriate teaching groups. However, is this an administrative job or one that requires the judgement of a teacher? If all it involves is processing lists of children then it is an administrative role and should not be done by a teacher at all. But if it involves deciding where a child's needs will be met in the most appropriate manner then it is a teacher's role. However, the outcomes of this aspect of the job are that pupils are:

   ■ actively participating in learning

   ■ taught in groups appropriately targeted to their stage of development

   ■ taught in appropriately structured groups.

   The outcome can also be phrased in terms of leadership and management of the department because managing setting is also about ensuring that members of the team have classes of an appropriate size and, as part of the school policy, have groups with a spread of attainment within a narrow range.

2 *Organising oral exams for GCSE* – again, is this an exercise in listing the names of children and giving them a time for their exam? If so, it shouldn't be done by a teacher. However, if it is about preparing materials for teachers to use with their classes, arranging for children to be prepared for the exams to a consistent standard then it is a teacher's role – and one that enables the role to address the oracy brief that the self-evaluation report highlighted for development. Therefore the outcomes of this aspect of the job are that pupils are:

   ■ prepared for oral examinations to a consistent standard

- able to speak with fluency on a specified range of topics
- able to use a range of phrases in oral examinations
- achieve grades commensurate with their target grade in oral exams.

The difference here is that the outcomes are specified in terms of what pupils will be able to do as a result of the work that the teacher will do. It is less about what activity the teacher will undertake and more about what the impact will be on the pupils. This is an important distinction between activity-based work and impact-focused work.

Having considered the outcomes of the role in terms of pupil progress, the job can be specified further by listing some of the tasks that are associated with the role.

The person specification

You should be in a position to write some kind of profile of the person that is required – a person specification. This profile sets out the kind of person that you are looking to recruit. It should be set out in the form of a list of skills and attributes that the appointee should possess. Examples of these are:

- a good honours graduate in . . . .
- experience of more than one school
- a commitment to teaching junior age children
- an interest in extracurricular activities
- a willingness to participate in the development of teaching schemes
- the ability to produce teaching resources.

An important point to note at this stage is that for every aspect of the person specification there should be an assessment stage. There are various elements to the assessment – the letter of application, application form, reference, evidence of qualifications, interview etc. – but the principle is that the person specification should drive the assessment process. Having decided on what sort of person you want – in terms of qualifications, experience, skills and attributes – the assessment process should enable you to determine the person who best fits the specification.

In some cases it may be useful to consider what is essential and what is desirable. For example, it may be desirable to recruit a good honours graduate in mathematics to fill a mathematics teaching post in a secondary school. However, the vagaries and uncertainties of recruitment for such posts may mean that such criteria may attract a very small field. Therefore, to set the essential criterion as 'an honours graduate in a mathematically-related discipline' with the 'good honours graduate in mathematics' as the desirable attribute may be more expedient. These are judgements you will make when consulting with the headteacher. However, it is bad advice to put something that you *really* regard as essential into the desirable column because if someone satisfies the 'essential' then they should be considered seriously for interview and ultimate appointment.

The objective of the person specification is to establish the kind of teacher the school is intending to appoint. It also provides the middle manager with the agenda of the recruitment process. Having composed such a document, it will drive the remainder of the process.

Producing the advertisement and the recruitment pack

The recruitment pack should contain the following as a minimum:

- the job description
- the person specification
- a copy of the advertisement
- some information about the school and department
- information about the job, such as the closing date and processes (i.e. when the interviews will be).

Your school may choose to include a letter from the headteacher, a copy of the prospectus, a copy of the OfSTED report, newsletters etc. If it is not your school's practice to include a letter from the headteacher, ask if you can write one to go into the pack.

The advertisement is clearly a very important piece of work – not only because it is very expensive to advertise, and getting it wrong is expensive, but also because it is the first contact that prospective colleagues have with the school.

There are a number of standard features in any advertisement and these are:

- the name and address of the school
- the name of the headteacher
- size of roll, age range and any specialism

- title of the advertised post and remuneration
- start date
- where to get further details and the closing date for applications.

Graphics and pictures increase the cost considerably and it may be that the school's budget allows for this but, typically, the need is to edit the amount of text rather than expand it. The text therefore has to be punchy and convey something of what you want and what you have to offer.

As part of the recruitment pack you need to have some information about the department. There may be a standard format used by your school but often it is up to the head of department to organise this.

It is worthwhile reflecting on what kind of information you would like to see if you were applying for the job. A good information sheet includes:

- a list of members of the team and their responsibilities
- results over the past three to five years
- teaching resources used – for example a purchased scheme of work or textbook resources
- the place of ICT in your programme of study
- extracurricular activities in the department
- numbers doing the subject at GCSE and A level
- department aims and values.

The objective is to give people sufficient information to help them to decide if they want to be part of your team. It is important to be honest about the department but in a positive manner so that people are encouraged to apply.

A contact number or e-mail address for further information shows that you are taking the process seriously and are keen to engage with your future colleague.

 Processing applications

As the applications arrive, you will want to collaborate with the headteacher in producing a longlist. Headteachers may have particular views on the role of the middle manager in the recruitment process – this may vary from being given a shortlist just a few days before the interviews to delegation of the entire process. However, it is reasonable to expect to be involved in:

- production of the advertisement
- compilation of the person specification and job description

- final shortlisting
- interviewing
- decision making.

The correct way to manage the longlisting process is to use the person specification. By constructing a grid which sets out all the criteria, it is possible to go through each application and assess it against the criteria. Some managers will use a points system for each criterion:

2 – strength
1 – some evidence
0 – no evidence.

At the end of the longlisting process there will be a rough rank order of candidates. The first group (say six) will be invited for interview – the remainder will be held as reserves. The advantage of this approach is that it is rigorous and fair. It means that if there is any question over the school's process, there is documentary evidence to support its methods. At this point the school may send for references.

Setting up and managing assessment days

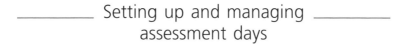

In setting up the interview day, several decisions need to be made and these will be discussed in turn.

Do you want the candidates to teach a class?

This practice varies a good deal and can depend on the subject. It can be quite daunting to have to teach a class before the panel who will be interviewing for the post. However, the advantages are that the panel gets to see how the candidate relates to children at first hand. Provided that the class is well chosen and the criteria for the lesson observation are made clear, the exercise can be valuable. It is better, in our view, for the candidates to suffer a few 'wobbles' and discomfort than for children's education to be affected by an unsuitable teacher.

This does call into question the validity of references, the extent to which they are reliable and how accurate a picture they give of a candidate's suitability for the job. In our view, the decision to ask candidates to teach can be one the middle manager takes, but it should be in the context of the whole-school recruitment process.

There are particular instances, however, where this can be varied. For example, if you are recruiting a PE teacher then a coaching session would be worthwhile; if a music teacher took an orchestra practice then the impression formed could be valuable for the recruitment process. This is a decision you should consider with care – and you should be aware of how you might feel in the same situation.

Do you want the candidates to perform a task?

The intention that underpins both teaching a lesson and performing a task is twofold. First, it is to find a way of getting beyond the application form – to find out more about the person. Second, it is attempting to validate the application form and the references. Is the person on the application form the person in front of us now?

There are tasks which can be set to facilitate this effectively and, used wisely, can provide a good basis for questions later on. It is a matter of choice and there are a range of things that you can ask people to do.

- *Presentation on a topic* – this enables you to assess an individual's presentation skills and determine their level of confidence with an audience. If there is a current topic then it is useful to assess how confident and informed the person is. However, if you are interviewing six people for a job then listening to six presentations all on the same topic is time-consuming, and very boring! If you are intending to choose between candidates after panel interviews then the presentation can be useful in discriminating.

- *Written answer to a question* – this enables you to assess the candidates' powers of expression and their ability to think on the spot. If this is going to be worthwhile there has to be time in the schedule for candidates to respond, and for the selection panel to read the responses.

- *Observed discussion* – this allows you to assess how well people interact with one another and their interpersonal skills – but it is an incredibly false situation.

- *Evaluation of a teaching resource* – the benefit of this approach is that you are able to relate the task to a teaching and learning situation and see the extent to which the person is focused on the job in question.

Whatever you decide to do, it is important that people are treated with dignity and that each element of the process clearly links with the person specification. The more assessment elements, the greater the validity of the process – but when giving feedback to candidates you will need to be able to comment on how well each performed in each task.

Do you intend to hold panel interviews only?

Panel interviews are those in which the candidates are interviewed by small groups of people, or alone. Typically, candidates will be interviewed by the middle manager (perhaps with a governor), a member of the leadership team and others. The panels will later come together and make a decision based on the candidates' performances in the interviews.

The advantages of this process are that, for people new to the profession, this can be less daunting than six or seven people firing questions at them. Also, people find it harder to mask any deficiencies in their application if the process is extended over a period of time. This is not to suggest that candidates deliberately mislead those who interview, but it must be recognised that when people want a job, they are capable of exaggeration and self-aggrandisement. The process which seeks to authenticate an application is called 'triangulation' – the application form is checked out using both the references and the interview questions. The principle is that when a candidate makes an assertion in their application, this is tested out by looking at the reference and by asking pertinent questions.

The disadvantage of panel interviews is that there is less control over the interview process and there is limited opportunity to see candidates answering questions on a range of topics. This illustrates the need for you to agree the process with the headteacher, so that the elements of the recruitment process are seen as complementary.

Will the process involve panel interviews followed by final interviews?

The advantage of following panel interviews with a final interview is that it addresses the deficiencies pointed out in the preceding section. The main disadvantage is time. A full recruitment process with tasks, panel interviews and final interviews will take up an entire day. However, this is time well spent if the end result is an appointment about which everyone is confident.

How will you inform candidates and what feedback will be offered to the unsuccessful?

Many readers will recall being kept in a room until the successful candidate was offered the job and then being offered feedback. Schools have changed their procedures in that candidates can be telephoned in the evening with the news. There are a number of advantages to this.

- There is not the pressure to make a decision quickly – knowing that there are five or six people sitting outside as the clock ticks by can force the pace unnecessarily.

- The preferred candidate can be offered the post and if it is declined the subsequently successful candidate need never know – we all like to think we were the first choice!

- The candidates have had time to distance themselves from the school and so will accept with surety – the emotion of an interview day can lead people to make decisions they later regret.

- Feedback can be offered without the rawness of the interview process having being recently concluded.

- It seems less brutal and more humane.

Again, these decisions will need to be taken at a school level, but it is important to have a view on these matters and be able to exercise the judgement they bring to the recruitment of the teacher to the team.

Telling people they have been unsuccessful is not very pleasant and people will react in a variety of ways. Our advice is to give people proper feedback – tell them, how they performed on each of the assessment tasks, the things they did well and the things they need to improve on. If people leave a selection process feeling that they have something on which they can work on and improve then it helps to mitigate the hurt that rejection inevitably brings. Again, your school may have its own ways of managing these situations – volunteering to tell people bad news may seem perverse but it is very good experience at managing a difficult situation.

Conducting interviews

Having decided the format for the recruitment process, the next matter to consider is how to conduct the interview itself. Generally speaking, newly appointed middle managers will have been on the sharp end of an interview process but being involved in the recruitment of a new team member for the first time can be quite daunting. The responsibility that goes with the decision-making process is understandable, but there are a number of pointers which can aid the task.

By focusing on the person specification, the agenda for the interview starts to draw together. However, the purpose of the interview needs to be explored. In the main, the appointing panel will have a body of information about each candidate. The task can be viewed as moving from information to possible interview questions. Table 5.3 gives some suggestions.

TABLE 5.3 Interview questions

Information and source	Areas for questions in the interview	Issues which arise
Educational background of the candidate	■ What characterised your own schooling?	■ Is this person in teaching as a response to their own experiences?
	■ What memories do you have of your own schooling?	■ Is the candidate reflective?
	■ What features of your own education do you bring to your work as a teacher?	■ Does the person look forward or back?
Subjects studied at school and university	■ Why did you choose to study . . . ?	■ Commitment to the subjects.
	■ What were the best things about studying . . . ?	■ Range of educational experience.
	■ Would you recommend a course in . . . ?	■ Ability to move from personal experience to advising students in school.
Teaching practice (or previous experience for subsequent teaching posts)	■ Describe your first teaching practice/post.	■ Does the person have significant experience?
	■ What did you learn from this?	■ Has the person learnt from their experience?
	■ Describe an incident which challenged your view of education.	■ Does the person refer matters appropriately?
	■ What is your teaching style?	■ Does the person have a view on what constitutes effective teaching? How

TABLE 5.3 *(cont'd)*

Information and source	Areas for questions in the interview	Issues which arise
		does this relate to their answers to questions on their own experience?
	■ What are the elements of a good lesson?	
Extracurricular involvement	■ What is your involvement in . . . ?	■ What is the person's view of education as a holistic experience?
	■ What do you think is the place of extracurricular activity?	■ Does the person have ideas?
	■ Who should be involved?	■ Is the person committed to the culture of the school?
	■ How can we increase the involvement in extracurricular activity?	
References	■ Does the reference support the application?	■ Do the application, references and responses triangulate?

Newly qualified teachers

There are particular issues when appointing a newly qualified teacher (NQT) which need to be considered. These are to do with recruitment, interviewing and induction.

It is beneficial to establish relationships, where possible, with education departments in universities and colleges of further education. Where there is a vacancy in the school which would suit an NQT, the appropriate department can advise on suitable candidates. The advantage of this is that, over time, colleges and schools can develop a mutually supportive relationship and teaching students can be suitably appointed. There is clearly a cost benefit too. Some schools with a large turnover will involve themselves in graduate fairs at universities, but this is less common.

Newly qualified teachers come to schools with enthusiasm and ideas, untainted by experience. The profile of NQTs has changed over the years to include people embarking on second careers. This can be as the result of lifestyle change brought on by redundancy, return to work etc. Thus, by seeking to appoint an NQT over a teacher with two or three years' experience, the team may not recruit the youngest person available. Our view is that appointment should not be on the basis of age alone – to do so would be discriminatory. The appointment process has to be fair and you have a responsibility to ensure that the processes used will stand up to inspection.

Some colleges of education are proactive about preparing their students to make applications and provide them with opportunities to do mock interviews. However, there is no substitute for the real thing and it is important to be sensitive to the needs of these young (at least in professional terms) people. A useful caveat when interviewing an NQT is to appoint on the basis of what they may be and what they appear to have to offer, rather than what they are at this time.

The overall framework for the interview process has to be designed to see what people can do and what they might offer the team and the school. The time spent on this will be rewarded only if the assessment techniques are appropriate to the profile being sought. Table 5.4 summarises the recruitment process.

TABLE 5.4 Summary of the recruitment process

To summarise, the recruitment process should:

- start with a team audit

- involve a person specification

- involve a job description

- advertise explicitly for the person required

- select on the basis of the person specification

- be fair, open and transparent – with each decision being justified and feedback to the candidates available

- provide opportunities for the candidates to demonstrate what they can offer

- facilitate the triangulation process to authenticate the candidates' responses.

Recruiting a deputy subject leader

The process of recruiting a deputy subject leader is, in many respects, similar to that required for recruiting any other member of the team. However, because of the close professional working relationship between the subject leader and the deputy, there is a greater emphasis on the person specification and its relationship to the team audit.

While the audit of skills and attributes will identify key characteristics which will need to be addressed in the recruitment process, it is important to appreciate that in recruiting a deputy subject leader you are, potentially, recruiting your successor and so using your own job description is a useful model for drawing up your deputy's.

To this end, therefore, the deputy subject leader will need to be developed to take on this whole-team role and they need to provide evidence that they have the ability to do this (in the future). Therefore, when analysing the applications for a deputy subject leader you need to consider the job description more closely.

TASK 18

Defining the role of the deputy subject leader

Consider the range of tasks you would expect a deputy subject leader to undertake.

The principles which underlie each job description are that:

- the postholder should be responsible to you, as line manager
- there should be administrative tasks
- there should be developmental tasks
- there should be opportunities for the postholder to develop managerial and leadership skills
- the job description should mirror that of the team leader.

The acid test of a job description is that the postholder should know exactly what they have to do and to whom they have to report. It should be a document of clarity and definition. While the contracting, that is a necessary part of effective delegation, is excluded from the job description, there is no doubt who is responsible for the delivery of the tasks set out.

To define a job description purely in administrative terms is poor practice because not only would it be very dull but it would not raise the standards of teaching and learning. Also, setting out a job description which is entirely administrative gives the middle manager a heavy burden in monitoring the work that is being done. However, there needs to be some administrative content because:

- it shares the load of administration across the team
- it frees the middle manager for other tasks
- it provides a range of experiences for the postholder to develop management skills.

The job description should be developmental in that it gives the postholder the opportunity to create and manage projects. Some projects can be far-reaching and wide-ranging depending on the type of school. A postholder who is, for example, deputy head of the junior section in a large primary school, might develop the personal, social and health education curriculum across the key stage. This would clearly be a major project which would give the postholder the opportunity to develop significant skills in:

- project planning
- project management
- the change process
- monitoring the work of others
- preparing reports for the line manager
- etc.

Such a job description would enable the postholder to develop skills to be able to move to a middle management role of their own in time.

In some teams it is possible for the deputy to have a job description which mirrors that of the middle manager. This is usually possible only in larger schools where there are more tasks to be undertaken. An example of this is where the head of subject has overall responsibility for the subject but specific responsibility for Key Stage 4; the deputy subject leader's job description mirrors this by having responsibility for Key Stage 3.

Appointing staff

Once a person has been offered and accepted a post both sides have entered into a legally binding contract – it is good practice to commit this agreement to paper but it doesn't change the binding nature of the offer and acceptance. It is up to you as the person's line manager to make contact with the successful candidate and to manage their induction.

The induction of new staff

Inducting a new member of the team

Frequently, the arrangements for the induction of a new member of staff is split between a member of staff with specific responsibility for this task (such as the staff development coordinator) and the line manager.

Schools are usually helpful in releasing a member of staff to spend a day at their new school for the purposes of induction, and the responsibility for the arrangements may fall on the middle manager.

The first principle is that the person should have a very pleasant day and leave the school pleased with the decision they made – maybe several months ago – and ready for the new role. This is best achieved by having a blend of activities and meetings, with some unstructured time for informal conversation and finding ways around the school and department.

An appropriate day could include the following.

- A meeting with the headteacher or member of the leadership team.
- Being presented with a copy of the timetable, class lists and other administrative material.
- Time to discuss any issues concerning classes.
- Being presented with a staff handbook, department handbook and schemes of work.
- Being presented with textbooks and other relevant teaching materials.
- Advice and guidance on staff procedures – where the toilets are, arrangements for lunch, where the photocopier is, accessing the school network etc.
- Meetings with colleagues – including tutor team leader, other members of the subject team etc.
- Fire and other health and safety procedures.

When the person starts working at the school then, in the absence of any formal induction process, there are several matters which are important to address with the new colleague. These include:

- INSET arrangements
- reporting and assessment at the school
- preparing for parents evenings

- briefing about important events
- tutorial arrangements
- staff working groups
- SEN arrangements.

If you take a proactive approach to arranging for your new colleague's induction then it will foster very good relationships for the future.

The most important aspect of induction is performance management and how this process is initiated. There is a temptation to wait for people to settle in for a period before you start actively monitoring their performance. In our view, *every* conversation with a colleague is about you monitoring their performance, and the best time to establish that relationship is right at the beginning. Therefore it is our advice that you arrange to meet with the person briefly at the end of the first day to check that all is well and formally after a week. At this meeting you can agree objectives and arrange for a lesson observation during the first period.

Monitoring the work of the new member of the team during the first few months

This is essential if the new member of the team is to get off to a good start. However, needs vary and there are a number of different scenarios to consider. We consider these using Tasks 19 and 20 and a case study.

TASK 19

Newly qualified teacher

Julia was appointed as an NQT in January during the first period of her teaching practice.

At interview, Julia was happy with the start that she had made on teaching practice, but her reference indicated that more effort should be given to lesson planning.

When Julia's final report was sent to school, as part of her induction pack, it was stated by the university that some classroom management problems had arisen because of the low expectations that Julia had of her classes.

How should you manage Julia during the first few months?

This is quite a sensitive one because there were some concerns about Julia when she was appointed, which have been substantiated during the teaching practice period. It is necessary therefore to be very clear with Julia that this kind of performance won't be good enough for her to be successful in her induction year. It is tempting to go straight in and ask her to present you with daily lesson plans, or otherwise use the alternative of giving her the benefit of the doubt and seeing how she gets on. There is a third way however. That is to have a meeting where you ask her to reflect on her experience on teaching practice and work through the target she had as part of her induction. By tactfully discussing the problem openly, you can make sure that she knows you are aware of the difficulties she experienced and provide her with sufficient support and challenge to make a fresh start putting right the mistakes she made on teaching practice. You will also have a 'backstop' position should the first few days and weeks reveal that more effort is required for lesson planning in the new context. If you then need to step up the process then there is scope for doing so. Failing to meet standards by the end of a teacher's induction year is professionally disastrous. Therefore, good records must be kept of meetings, support and interventions. Doing this is a professional responsibility you have to the students, the teacher and, of course, the profession. Hopefully it will be fine but it is necessary to prepare for the possibility that it might not work out for the teacher.

TASK 20

Fast tracking

Tim is a history teacher on the DfES *FastTrack* programme. As such he is paid an additional increment and there is a requirement that he gets involved in whole school projects.

Tim isn't sure just what he will be doing or what will be expected of him during the first year.

How should you manage Tim during the first few months?

People on the DfES *FastTrack* programme get paid an additional increment and are expected to take on additional projects so that they develop the skills and experiences to progress quickly through the profession. However, the demands of the classroom are considerable for a new teacher, and it is important that in the first period there is no distraction from the core function of being a classroom teacher. This may be a difficult course to steer if you have a teacher who is very keen to get on and wants to do lots of things. Clearly, individuals vary but it is unlikely that an NQT will have acquired the necessary skills and experiences before the end of the first semester to start to look outside their own classroom. It is necessary to plan the programme with a teacher – and *FastTrack* teachers have a mentor on the leadership team who will guide this aspect of their role. The support and guidance offered, and the insistence that they become the best teacher possible, will be good advice.

TASK 21

Teaching support

Jordan is a newly appointed curriculum administrator to the department. Her role is to provide technical support to your department. She will do all the filing, produce standard letters and produce materials for teachers.

She hasn't worked in a school before but is a very proficient administrator.

How will you manage Jordan during the first few months?

Whenever a new person joins a team it is really very important that they feel part of the team and that they are needed. Part of the challenge of the national remodelling has been to develop new roles in school – but it is *people* that make them a success or otherwise. Briefing the team to ensure that any Luddism is countered is vital. People aren't always very keen to have work taken away from them which they regard as pleasurable – although it might be boring, repetitive, mindless and anathema to teaching and learning! One consequence is that people like Jordan end up feeling unwanted and not trusted to do their jobs. Briefing the team accordingly and ensuring that for the first period she has plenty to do, including some of your own administrative tasks, will help her to settle in.

 Summary

The principles for induction apply to everyone who joins the team. It is important that they are given the opportunity to settle in and feel part of the team. It is equally vital, however, that you take the opportunity to set the agenda for future working relationships by meeting regularly, focusing on the person's core function and providing them with feedback from the earlier opportunity.

chapter six

Dads and lads, girls and their mums

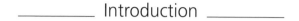

Introduction

Working with parents and managing students are two of the most important areas of the manager's role. They are also the areas where it is possible to get things spectacularly wrong, ending up being a problem with a teacher, a student and a parent. In this chapter we are going to think about the various dimensions to the relationships and how they can be managed in a proactive manner.

Managing behaviour is one of those areas that can always be improved and is always subject to random events. For most of us who work in comprehensive schools, managing behaviour is high on the list of important activities – not because standards are lower than in other types of schools but simply because the inclusion agenda has increased the demands on schools and broadened the range of young people who make up the school population. Many teachers in grammar schools enjoy very high standards of student behaviour but children can be merciless with a weak teacher, and unforgiving of a teacher who is unprepared or not in command of their subject. Managing student behaviour is an issue for us all.

The first point to make is that successful behaviour management is principally about effective teaching and learning. Most classrooms are peaceful, well-managed places because teaching is the best it can be. The learning needs of children have been taken into account and the teacher has planned the activities accordingly. The children are kept busy with plenty of interesting, varied and appropriate work underpinned by clear direction and good relationships. In short, get the teaching right and the problems are few.

However, it is not always quite that straightforward. As the head of department or head of year you will be managing the behaviour of children outside your own classes. Hence, you are one step removed from the initial situation and therefore your response has to be different. You will be dealing with problems that have occurred in someone else's classrooms or at times of the day when you might be in another part of the school – but you will need to respond in some way. As with all the issues that we face in our schools, the best way is to take a team approach and to work through the questions together and agree a way forward.

Much of what you will have to do is reactive – you will have to deal with some students only because of what they have done or failed to do. There are some circumstances where you can anticipate potential difficulty, but when it is someone else's class it becomes a greater challenge.

One of the most important skills for any teacher is to be able to deal with students effectively. The characteristics of the relationships between a teacher and students vary and can either reflect or run counter to the culture of the school. Some schools are characterised by warm relationships where there is easy and relaxed interaction across all levels. In many schools the teaching staff will be on first name terms with the headteacher – in few schools will students be on first name terms with their teachers. Some schools insist on or encourage use of the terms 'Sir', 'Madam' or 'Miss' when students address their teachers, and some will prefer the name to be used. There are still some schools – mainly boys schools – where students are called by their surnames. The purpose of this discussion is not to offer a critique of the 'name-calling' but to provide a context for one of the most challenging tasks for a manager, and that is to deal with students. The manager will have to deal with students when a teacher has become unable or unwilling to do so. The teacher may have exhausted all their own strategies for managing the student. All the strategies that the team structure offers may have been used. It is at this point that the manager will have to deal with the student personally.

What sets this task apart from others is the need to deal with someone else's problems in such a way that the teacher is not disempowered or does not lose face. This is set against the paradox that, as leader, you may not have anyone to deal with those students in your class who exhaust *your* strategies. This will be considered later in the chapter.

The purpose of this chapter is to consider why it is important to have an effective policy on behaviour management and how the manager can empower the team to deal more effectively with their students. It also addresses the need for appropriate intervention by the manager and how to manage this. This is in the context of managing student learning and progress.

 Behaviour management

The first question to ask is, what is behaviour management? Clearly behaviour management in the team situation is affected by the overall approach in the school. However, an effective head of department or head of year will manage students in a manner reflecting the team's approach to learning. Behaviour management is about making sure that students are able to learn and that teachers are able to teach – it is as simple and complex as that. Behaviour management therefore needs to be considered in the context of the school policy and at a team level.

Within the context of the school

Many schools will have a behaviour policy and this will include statements, referring to the following.

- *The start of lessons* – for example, students will be silent for the register, will remove outdoor coats, will take out books and write in the date, apologise for lateness etc.

- *During the lesson* – students will pay attention, do their best, raise a hand to ask or answer questions, respect others etc.

- *End of lessons* – students will write down homework in their diary, pack up quietly, leave as instructed.

- *Between lessons* – students will walk on the left of the corridor, observe the one-way system etc.

These will be familiar to most schools where such a policy exists. It is not uncommon for this policy to be synthesised into a 'code of conduct' – or some other name – and this to be posted in all classrooms. The first responsibility for the manager, therefore, is to check, if required, that the policy be posted in the team's classrooms. Further, if there are actions set out in the policy – such as taking the register at the start of each lesson – that this is checked as part of the monitoring process. If a team is seen to observe the policy and that the manager monitors the policy, then issues can be managed in an unobtrusive way.

Within the team

There may be issues, affecting the subject team or the pastoral team, which may require additions to be made to the school policy. These may include:

- the teaching of the subject
- the practical nature of the subject
- the use of equipment and resources
- the accommodation.

The implications for each of these circumstances are outlined in Tables 6.1–6.4.

TABLE 6.1 The teaching of the subject

Feature	Implications for behaviour management	Implications for the manager
The subject requires a high level of teacher exposition.	■ Teachers will need to be perceptive when planning lessons which require large amounts of exposition. ■ Students may need to be seated according to a seating plan. ■ Students may be seated facing the board – when the teacher writes on the board her back is to the class.	■ Staff may need guidance when planning such lessons to enable them to balance the time spent listening and writing. ■ Staff may need guidance on the appropriate manner in which students create notes – copying from the board, from a book, use of photocopied worksheets etc. ■ Teachers may need guidance on the efficacy of seating plans and how they can be used to manage behaviour. ■ The manager may need to offer guidance to teachers on dealing with minor misbehaviour, according to the team strategy. ■ The manager may have to deal with students whose misbehaviour is a consequence of a high level of exposition.
Students need to work occasionally in groups.	■ Students may be unused to group work – either as a whole or within the subject. ■ The classroom space may inhibit group work.	■ Staff may need to be trained in the effective use of group work. ■ The use of group work may need to be debated as a teaching strategy. Consequently, group work may be introduced gradually and its contribution to effective learning monitored. ■ The manager may have to respond to students who find group work difficult or where it has been managed poorly by the teacher.

TABLE 6.1 (cont'd)

Feature	Implications for behaviour management	Implications for the manager
Students need to discuss – as a class or in groups.	■ Eye contact between students when sitting in rows facing the board is difficult and may inhibit good discussion.	■ Class discussion is an acquired skill. It demands very effective control and the ability to include all members of the class. When students are discussing in groups, these demands are emphasised. The manager may have to deal with students who misbehave because their contributions are inappropriate or the discussion is ineffectively managed.
Students need to write for extended periods.	■ The furniture needs to be adequate for this purpose.	■ Students may be unused or unable to write for extended periods and this may result in poor behaviour, which the teacher may refer to the manager.
The subject may make occasional or extensive use of visual and/or aural teaching aids.	■ Students need to be able to see a screen or television. ■ Students need to be able to hear a recording (the acoustics may be problematic). ■ The room may have to be darkened to show films etc.	■ Misbehaviour can occur when there is a change to the normal pattern. ■ Students may be referred to the manager because the management of this teaching process has failed in some way.
The subject may have a high oral component.	■ Procedures for asking and answering questions are needed.	■ The skills required of the teacher are great in this setting. The teacher needs to be able to control the class in such a way that contributions are managed. The manager may need to train staff to do this effectively and deal with students whose behaviour is inappropriate.

TABLE 6.2 The practical nature of the subject

Feature	Implications for behaviour management	Implications for the manager
Students work on individual projects at varying stages of completion – e.g. Paintings, models, textiles, food etc.	■ Students finish at different times – some students may distract others if bored. Slower students may become disaffected.	■ Students may be referred to the manager because of disaffection or boredom.
Students may work in groups and need to prepare to perform – e.g. sequences in dance, episodes in drama, compositions in music, plays in English etc.	■ Students may not be focused on the task and might use the task as an opportunity to misbehave. ■ Students may not work well in groups. ■ Problems which have occurred outside the class may be given space to develop in a group work situation.	■ The team may require training on effective group work and project management. ■ Conflicts may arise because of the group dynamics – the teacher may not be aware of the circumstances, which have caused the conflict.
The class may be noisy, of necessity.	■ Proximity of other classrooms may restrict practical work. ■ The teacher may find it difficult to gain attention. ■ Some noise may not be linked to the work being done.	■ Other staff may complain about the noise and disturbance.
There may be no written work produced during the lesson or series of lessons.	■ Students may devalue the work and treat it with less respect.	■ This is an assessment issue which needs to be considered when organising such work.

TABLE 6.3 The use of equipment and resources

Feature	Implications for behaviour management	Implications for the manager
Equipment may have to be shared between classes or among groups of students.	■ Equipment may need to be moved from one area to another. Insufficient equipment may necessitate different lesson planning. ■ Behaviour issues may arise because of the need to share equipment.	■ The manager may wish to set up a booking system for the use of resources and delegate this task. There may be a need for training in the efficient use of the resources. ■ If there are behaviour issues resulting from the need to share equipment then alternative learning experiences may have to be considered.
Equipment may be potentially hazardous.	■ Health and safety procedures will need to be in place. The behaviour policy for the subject should reflect the hazardous nature of the materials being used.	■ The manager is commonly responsible for health and safety procedures in their domain. There is a need to identify the first aid person and to specify in the team handbook the precise personal responsibilities for Health and Safety. This could be part of each teacher's job description – for example 'The teacher is responsible for advising the manager in writing of any breakdown in the fabric which might constitute a health and safety risk'.
Resources may be expensive.	■ The policy of the school may need to be developed to take account of the misuse of expensive resources. ■ If equipment and resources are at such a premium that the teacher has to demonstrate a process – for example an experiment in science – there are behaviour issues that need to be considered when preparing such a lesson.	■ Students may be referred to the manager where resources have been wasted or misused.

TABLE 6.4 The accommodation

Feature	Implications for behaviour management	Implications for the manager
Crowding in a corridor	■ In most secondary schools, students move from one subject to another at the change of lesson. This usually necessitates moving from one part of the building to another – there can be over a thousand people on the move. This can have implications for behaviour management in that teachers need to ensure that students move quickly and safely. ■ The start of a lesson can be untidy because groups of students may arrive at different times. ■ The system may be such that students wait outside a classroom until the teacher is present.	■ The manager will have to monitor the dismissal of classes and ensure that this happens on time. Further, there is a need, particularly in this situation, for the team to be punctual and alert to the difficulties this situation creates. It is important, however, that this is seen as an area the manager can control, if the team is efficiently deployed. ■ Teachers will need training to equip them with skills to enable them to start the lesson, despite some of the class being late. Also, there may need to be some negotiation with the teacher from the previous lesson to minimise the time lost. ■ The manager may organise staff to patrol the corridors to encourage good behaviour.
Entrances and exits	■ This may be problematic as students try to leave the area and others try to enter.	■ The manager may wish to organise the supervision of entrances and exits. ■ The manager may impose a one-way system in their area.
Classroom use	■ The classrooms may be too small for classes to be there. This is a particular issue in schools where class sizes have grown considerably. This may affect the teaching methods used.	■ The manager may need to offer guidance on how to manage large classes in small classrooms.
Siting of the team classrooms	■ The subject area may be a long way from the area where students have had their previous lesson. ■ The team may not be suited to certain areas.	■ When the school timetable is being constructed, the manager needs to raise these issues – especially where it has the potential to disrupt the team's work.

_____ The manager's role _____

Having considered the issues that can affect behaviour management, it is important to consider the role that the manager plays in this area. There are several issues to consider. Their role is to support the teacher and to empower them to take appropriate action. This is not the same as doing their work for them. The following Case Study illustrates this point.

CASE STUDY

The class from hell

It is November. Miss Jones has been teaching at the school for five years and is a good teacher.

She has found her Year 9 class difficult to control, particularly on Thursdays, last lesson. She describes them to you as 'the class from hell'. She says that they don't listen to her and that they fail to come to lunchtime detentions.

This is the first time she has referred this class to you.

The temptation might be to go to the class and give them a telling off. There are several disadvantages to this approach.

- If it works, it will be because of your authority not that of Miss Jones. She may be seen as a person who can only control her class if she has someone to support her.

- As the manager you may have to leave your class to go to speak to Miss Jones' class.

- This approach does not solve the problem – it merely treats the symptoms.

- Miss Jones has not had to do anything to help herself, and as such has not considered her own role in this problem.

- Miss Jones still has no strategy to deal with this problem herself.

- The next time such a problem occurs, she will probably repeat her request for help.

As an alternative, a discussion with Miss Jones could be held and strategies agreed. The discussion should address the following issues.

- When she says 'all the class' does she really mean *all* of the children or are there individuals who are responsible for leading the disorder.

- Is this behaviour typical of the class or is their conduct different at other times of the week?

- What work is she setting them to do? Is the work appropriate? Is the work matched to their abilities?

- How does she react to minor misbehaviour? What sanctions does she use?

- How can she plan the lesson to reduce the misbehaviour? How should she respond to minor misbehaviour? Is there a case for removing students temporarily (to an assigned place) or placing certain students on team report?

The outcomes of this meeting should be that:

- the head of department should understand the problem – but the problem remains with Miss Jones

- Miss Jones should be equipped with strategies to address the problem

- the head of department should articulate the support they will offer

- the head of department should state how they will monitor the work of the class and what reports are needed from Miss Jones – this may be in the form of weekly reports etc.

- there should be a review of the strategy at an appropriate time.

Managers should be prepared for the fact that students will be sent to them while they are teaching their own classes. The following Case Study illustrates what needs to be considered.

CASE STUDY

When disruptions intrude

You are teaching your Year 10 class. They are a good class and you have worked hard to establish good working habits. They are making excellent progress.

There are some difficult students in the class. You are in the middle of explaining a particularly difficult concept to the class – they are struggling with the material and you need to complete your explanation before they can do the next piece of work.

A student arrives at your classroom saying that Mr Lee has sent him to you. He has no work with him.

It is tempting to stop teaching and deal with the boy. However, there are disadvantages to this approach.

- The boy learns that by misbehaving he can gain the attention not only of his teacher (Mr Lee) but also the head of department.
- The boy has an audience. If he is in a bad temper, there is potential for further conflict. At best, he will not wish to lose face with other students looking on.
- The momentum of your own lesson will be disrupted. Your own class may then misbehave.
- The learning opportunity you have created will be affected and the progress your students are able to make may be compromised.

An alternative approach is to:

- tell the boy to sit down at a nominated desk – preferably in a place away from the gaze of others
- continue with the lesson
- at an appropriate moment give the boy a piece of paper and tell him to write a statement detailing what happened to cause him to be sent out of class
- at the end of the lesson arrange to see the boy to discuss what has happened and what will need to happen before his next lesson
- speak with Mr Lee – refer to the department policy which states that anyone sent to you must have some work to do
- resolve the conflict between Mr Lee and the student.

The advantages of this approach are that, as manager, you are seen to support the teacher but you demonstrate that you are not going to let the misbehaviour of another student affect the progress of your own. Also, it is very easy for a conflict between a teacher and a student to transfer into a conflict between the manager and the student. This approach avoids this potential.

CASE STUDY

The difficult pupil

Mrs Hodge is an excellent teacher. She has complained to you about a student called Louise in her class.

Her behaviour is poor. She disrupts the work of others and Mrs Hodge is finding it very hard to cope with the extremes of Louise's behaviour. Last lesson she was stabbing other children with her pen. Louise was rude when challenged by Mrs Hodge.

Mrs Hodge asks for help.

This is a situation where one student is affecting the progress of another and there is need for action on behalf of the manager. There are a number of possible approaches.

- Ask Mrs Hodge to document all the instances where Louise has misbehaved over the past two weeks. This will provide you with evidence on which you can judge the severity of the situation.

- Arrange to see Louise, with Mrs Hodge – at this meeting she should explain her behaviour, and you should state the actions you intend to take.

- Further actions might include excluding Louise from classes until a meeting with her parents is arranged, placing Louise on some kind of behaviour contract, discussing with the year leader whether Louise's behaviour is poor elsewhere.

- It is important to involve Mrs Hodge, up to a point. Mrs Hodge still has the responsibility for Louise's progress in the subject but it may be considered that the behaviour is so extreme and unacceptable that it is now the head of department's responsibility to deal with the student.

- The need for an effective policy is once more emphasised.

———— Developing a behaviour policy ————

It is vital for any manager to develop an effective strategy to manage behaviour for a number of reasons.

- Teachers need to be supported in their work.

- A manager's status is enhanced by effective strategy.

- Managers have a responsibility and without a strategy will find the management of their own classes difficult if they have to deal with other problems.

- An effective manager is proactive in these matters. A proactive approach reduces inconsistency and stress.

The first stage in developing a strategy is perhaps to do some kind of survey where the concerns of the team can be expressed. This can be done as part of a team meeting when members can be asked to identify the three main student behaviours which disrupt their teaching. The following examples could be given:

■ students being late

■ students failing to bring equipment

■ students calling out

■ students being rude.

Alternatively this could be in the form of a list, which the manager displays on a flip chart. The behaviours can then be classified in some way. The categories might include:

■ procedural – for example, students are required to be silent at the start of class for the register

■ punctuality and attendance

■ subject specific procedural – failure to bring kit, special equipment

■ behavioural – during whole-class teaching

■ behavioural – while the class is working.

There are several others that might be included. The objective of producing such a set of categories is that it enables the manager to develop strategies, which address particular issues. While it may be frustrating for the teacher if students are late for a lesson, it is not as bad as a student who cannot work as part of a group, in a subject where high levels of group work are a necessity. From this list of categories the team can consider what actions should be taken, and at what point the manager needs to intervene, if at all. Examples of these strategies are given in Table 6.5.

The crucial outcomes from such a meeting are that:

■ the team knows exactly what to expect from their manager

■ the responsibility for behaviour management remains with the classteacher, with the manager providing support – this means that even when a student is sent out of class, work is still set and the academic progress is still the class teacher's responsibility

■ once the manager intervenes it becomes their responsibility to deal with the student

■ in return for this support the team provides information – important evidence – and manages the setting of work.

TABLE 6.5 Strategies for tackling poor behaviour

Behaviour	Team strategy	Manager strategy
Lateness to class.	■ Students are required to apologise and explain their lateness. ■ If persistent lateness is a problem, investigate to find out if there is a valid excuse – for example, students travel from one side of the campus to another. ■ Breaktime detention to make up the time.	■ The manager might have to refer the problem to another colleague – for example, if the class is late from a practical lesson.
Students talk during class register.	■ Students write out the department policy (or school policy) during a breaktime.	■ Some staff might need support with this action.
Student talks while teacher is talking.	■ Teachers should have strategies for gaining and securing class control.	■ The manager discusses such strategies as part of the department's development.
Student fails to work in the prescribed manner.	■ If the behaviour is such that the learning outcomes of the class are compromised, the student might be given a task to do away from the others.	■ The manager might intervene if such a pattern continues.
Student fails to obey instructions.	■ One warning given and if student fails to comply, the student is sent to the manager with work to do. ■ The teacher writes a report of the incident.	■ The manager needs to ensure that there is a nominated place where students can be sent. This may necessitate the delegation of this role at times when the manager is unavailable. ■ The manager would require a meeting with the teacher and student to discuss future action.
Student assaults another student.	■ School policy usually covers such matters – at the very least the manager would remove the student from class. ■ The teacher writes a report of the incident.	■ The student is excluded from class until the matter is resolved.
Student abuses materials.	■ The matter is referred to the manager.	■ The manager writes to parents requesting payment for materials.

Monitoring behaviour

An effective means of monitoring the behaviour of students is to use some form of report. Placing a student on a report might result from persistent misbehaviour, persistent failure to produce homework or following a serious incident. Again, the use of such a system needs to be considered as part of the policy. The report should contain the following features:

- the name and tutor group of the student
- the name of the student's teacher
- a space for the teacher to comment on the student's behaviour – a separate space should be allocated for the teacher to comment on the quality of the work produced
- a list of targets – for example, to arrive to class with a full set of equipment, to remain on task for the specified time, to raise a hand before speaking
- a space for parental comment and signature
- a space for the manager to comment.

To maximise the potential of such a report there are a number of considerations.

- The use of targets – the targets should specify what the student has to do to make their behaviour acceptable.
- The report should be used as a short-term strategy with specified review date – for example, for four weeks.
- The student should know what will happen by failing to comply – for example, will be sent to the manager – and what will happen if the review is poor.
- Both student and parents should accept the targets and sign to acknowledge this.
- The report targets should be written so that they are personal to the student and that there is a good chance of success – this can be done quickly if the manager has a standard report pro forma, for example as a Word document, and inserts the targets.

Managing behaviour
as a manager

Most managers find that their status is useful as a means of managing behaviour. By setting out a policy and a system for dealing with those who misbehave, managers can establish themselves in this role. It can, however, be a lonely business – in setting up a system in which referrals are made to you, there is a presumption that you have no need of support yourself. It is important that in the first few weeks of the new role managers establish themselves as people who have effective strategies. However, many managers teach the most difficult classes so there is a need to negotiate support with the leadership team in the way that the manager negotiates support with their own team. If the structure is such that the manager can utilise support from team members then this can be very beneficial because it demonstrates trust and humility. Staff may accept support more readily if they see you, as a manager, using the strategies you are expecting them to use.

These matters are not easy to discuss. They cut to the heart of interpersonal and teaching skills. Where the teaching is well managed the need for behaviour management systems is lessened, in some respects. However, it is because the strategies are in place that effective teaching can be organised and the learning outcomes are the focus of the teacher's attention.

Working with parents – how to get them on your side

Working with parents should always be your first priority. This chapter is mainly about being proactive in resolving issues and preventing problems getting worse, but, of course, for the vast majority of children getting it right is what they want to do.

Working with parents adds a very important dimension to managing a successful team.

Firstly, thinking about the positive aspects, parents want to know how their children are getting along and it is an important part of your role to ensure that they get regular information that is robust and reliable. Keeping parents informed about their child's progress gives you the opportunity to build relationships with them and should difficulties arise there is then a positive basis for the interaction. Similarly, if there are changes to an examination specification, coursework requirements or any other aspect of the work of the team that will affect their child it is good practice to communicate with them. A significant number of schools have subject information evenings – the purpose being to inform parents of changes affecting the work of their children. Working proactively with parents to give them the opportunity to support the school is good practice.

Secondly, when you are working through the department rewards policy it is a good idea to think about how contact with parents will be made. Having a system in which letters, postcards or telephone calls are made to parents when their children do well is a really nice way to reinforce the good work that children do.

Parents' evenings

These are a really good opportunity to discuss a child's progress. Of course, this is when all the work on curriculum planning, assessment and rewards comes to the fore because all your team will be able to speak with authority and conviction. Such evenings are usually organised so that parents have a short five or ten minute meeting with each teacher to discuss progress. A well organised department will have all the necessary information to hand. It is important that this opportunity to raise serious issues with parents is taken. It is a waste of time if the meeting is filled with platitudes and inanities when there is a real problem to be tackled. However, being tactful with parents is very important – they are not the ones who have done something wrong (and even if they are, tactful ways need to be found to tell them!). Making parents feel that they are being treated as if they are naughty pupils doesn't move the relationship on very far. By being tactful, yet assertive and sticking to the facts – for example, how many homework assignments have been missed, or quoting instances of poor behaviour – you can engage the support of the parents to good effect.

As team leader you will sometimes find it necessary to contact parents to raise concerns about a pupil – often to support a colleague who is having difficulties with a student. A politely written letter explaining briefly the reason why it is important that you meet is a good start. School procedures vary, but it is our advice that you show this letter to a senior member of staff before you send it out. There may be mistakes in it and their experience may enable them to give advice or intelligence on this or any other issues with the parent or child. Sometimes, parents raise matters with the headteacher and ask that it is kept confidential – and inappropriate contact might cause a difficulty.

The principles involved in holding meetings with parents are as follows.

■ Be clear about the purpose of the meeting – explain to parents why you have asked for the meeting and have all the necessary supporting evidence (mark book, child's exercise book etc.)

- Organise the venue – make it welcoming and professional. If you need a room then make sure it is booked so that you can get the meeting off to a good start and appear to be well organised and professional.

- Be clear about what outcome you want – if you want a child to apologise, to do a detention or repeat a piece of work be clear in your own mind about what you want.

- If the parent has sought the meeting because they are unhappy, think about what the outcome needs to be – an apology from a teacher, re-marking of a piece of work, someone to say that a mistake was made etc.

- Anticipate difficulties – how has it reached the stage where a meeting is required? Is this because there was some problem at school, something wrong in your department or some breakdown in communication? Thinking about these aspects and what the response could be helps to give you confidence if matters become intractable.

- Be prepared to give ground if necessary – saying sorry is always a good place to start.

- Follow up the meeting with a letter and action – summarise what was discussed, acknowledge the difficulties and restate the way you have agreed to resolve them.

Hopefully, by planning the meeting you will be able to manage the situation successfully. It goes without saying that if the parent becomes violent, aggressive or abusive then it is advisable to conclude the meeting rather than risk an unpredictable outcome. The possibility of such an outcome has to be considered – hence our advice that you talk to a member of the leadership team about the meeting, just in case.

Summary

This chapter has been about managing the behaviour of students. Thinking about the way your department works and how students feel when they are working in it is a good place to start. How you take account of the views of learners, parents and carers when making plans is an increasingly important layer of accountability that has been brought to the fore recently. Students are people and as they rub along together with their teachers then things will go wrong – the effective team leader sees this as being part of the job. Having difficult issues to resolve can sometimes be unpleasant and can be the source of much distress and upset.

However, the teachers are the paid professionals who all have choices, but children *have* to come to school and must do what their teachers tell them.

It is too easy for teachers, at whatever level, to refer matters to a more senior colleague. A balance has to be found between resolving matters at team level and asking for a member of the leadership team to sort it out. An effective teacher believes in their own authority as a teacher – students do as they are required by an effective teacher because they respect that person. This respect is founded on high quality teaching and the understanding that the individual child matters. An effective head of department or head of year believes in their own authority as the leader of the team – the basis for that relationship is at another level, but fundamentally it relies on being fair.

chapter seven

How was it for us?

– department planning and self-evaluation

This chapter is about development planning. It is about how you move from an idea to a detailed plan that will enable you and the team to deliver.

_____ The autonomous department _____

The department team has to be part of the whole-school structure – hopefully, such a principle is unarguable. The idea of a department that is able to function in a completely different way from the rest of the school is one that we should not entertain – although we can recall departments that have been relatively successful in struggling schools.

However, in the same way that schools can have an earned autonomy, it is useful to think about the way in which a department team can develop this principle – and indeed why it should want to.

Firstly, being autonomous means having the freedom to innovate, to be self-governing and self-determining. This does not mean that the department team can do as it pleases – it is a very high level of accountability and responsibility based on a team that has clear principles and knows itself well. There are a number of elements that are essential prerequisites for this level of autonomy – we will explore these later in this chapter.

It is difficult to conceptualise what an autonomous department looks like, and to consider this more fully we are going to use a model of an autonomous school and make the necessary adjustments (see Table 7.1). This model is adapted from the Seattle Schools model for autonomous schools (see www.wshs.seattleschools.org for further information).

TABLE 7.1   Seven attributes of the autonomous department

---

1 *Common focus* – the autonomous department is one in which the staff and students have a shared vision and focus on what constitutes effective teaching and learning. In the autonomous department, all the decisions that need to be taken are governed by this shared vision. Put simply, the department team has clarity about what it is aiming to do, where it wants to be and how it knows what is happening.

2 *Personalisation* – the autonomous department is one that provides a rigorous and challenging curriculum to all students regardless of their aptitude, while supporting learning to help to ensure that students have the resources to succeed. The autonomous department is able to demonstrate that it is addressing the needs of the students at the individual level.

TABLE 7.1 *(cont'd)*

3 *A healthy and supportive culture* – the autonomous department is one that is characterised by a team that is responsive to the concerns of all stakeholders – students, staff, parents and the community alike – in its planning, delivery and evaluation.

4 *Academic rigour and high expectations* – the autonomous department is one that is driven by a deep interest in how students are progressing – the department will be able to say with authority what students know, are able to do and understand. The department is driven by accountability, allowing staff and students to take responsibility for learning in ways that allow them to respond to areas of student need while making available learning experiences that offer greater depth and authenticity.

5 *Effective curriculum planning and delivery* – the autonomous department uses its expertise to ensure that its planning is of the highest standard and is the result of collaborative working.

6 *Flexibility* – the autonomous department is sufficiently self-disciplined that it is able to develop programmes specifically to address the needs of individual students who present particular challenges; both the very able and the lower attaining.

7 *Learning partnerships* – the autonomous department structures itself in such a manner that it can partner other departments in the school, departments in other schools or employers and other stakeholder groups.

Being autonomous – where the department is trusted to plan, organise and evaluate its own work – represents a high ideal. It doesn't mean that the department is left completely on its own and can expect to be free from any accountability – it is in sharp contrast to this. It does mean that the team can be the authority on its work, and will welcome quality assurance as an opportunity to test out its self-evaluation processes and validate its judgements.

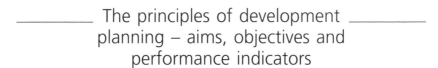

The principles of development planning – aims, objectives and performance indicators

The first part of this process is to have effective planning processes – in the next section we consider how to actually draw up a development plan.

There are a number of elements that go into making an effective development plan – performance indicators, aims, primary objectives, secondary objectives, desired outcome, timing, budget, responsibility and accountability.

Performance indicators

It is very easy to write a development plan that has success criteria that are completely pointless. For example, if the objective is to produce a set of keywords to address the literacy demands of the history curriculum, then the success criterion is that the keywords are produced. This criterion is perfectly sound in that if the keywords are produced then the criterion has been met. However, it is pointless because it does not require any analysis of the impact on student learning. It is important that the keywords are produced – because if the planned actions are not undertaken to completion then this leads to slippage for the plan as a whole – but in evaluative terms it is insufficient. Further, there is rarely one single action that will lead to improvement in pupil attainment. Having performance indicators that are distinct from the plan is an appropriate way to link the two, but not to reduce the plan to one that is evaluated only in terms of activity rather than impact. The performance indicators for a subject department in a secondary school could be as follows:

- Key Stage 3 level 5+ by gender
- Key Stage 3 level 6+ by gender
- SEN progress at all levels and stages
- GCSE A*–C for the department and by group
- GCSE A*–G for the department and by group
- Recruitment to AS and A2 courses
- GCE A–C and A–E grades at AS and A2 levels.

Aims

Separating aims and objectives can be difficult. Aims are overarching and objectives are the steps that you will take to realise the aim. So an appropriate aim might be to 'raise attainment of the most able students in French' or to 'raise attainment of all students' or to 'be an efficient department that offers value for money'. The aim is an overarching theme that will be realised through a series of activities and interventions.

Primary objectives

The next stage in the plan is to have a series of primary objectives that are going to realise the overarching aim. The rationale for primary and secondary objectives is that a secondary objective is the way in which a primary objective is to be delivered. Rarely can a primary objective just be actioned – it needs a set of smaller steps that will accumulate. To pursue the aim 'to raise attainment of the most able students in French', the primary objective might be to 'have a well-planned programme of study that addresses the needs of the most able'. This is an objective because you will, at the end of the process, either have a well-planned programme or not. Of course what makes for a 'well-planned programme of study' is an issue that needs to be explained in terms of the criteria – which follow on from this section.

Secondary objectives

These follow on from the primary objectives and are the smaller steps that enable the team to meet the objective. So, pursuing the objective to have a well-planned programme of study, there will be a series of steps which might include an overview by key stage, a year-by-year overview, term-by-term overview, lesson-by-lesson plans, production and/or purchase of specific resources etc. It is important at this stage to really think about every step that needs to be taken to realise an objective so that nothing gets forgotten – and also so that you are clear about the scale of the task ahead. Noting down that resources have to be purchased may seem trivial or pedantic, but these things all have a time component, and indeed a financial one. And, of course, it then requires the team to consider the lead times for production or purchase and any attendant issues.

Desired outcome

The team debate and set down what the desired outcome will be and identify any success criteria. How will you know if the programme of study is well planned? This is a very useful matter for discussion as agreeing what it will look like enables the team to work with clarity and purpose once the plan is agreed. Generally a programme of study will have individual lesson plans, with specific learning outcomes – each lesson plan will have a class set of resources, homework assignments, tests and other assessment materials.

Timing

Having been very precise about the secondary objectives – each of the small steps having been specified – you can then assign dates by which the actions have to be completed. Our preference is to be really specific and to align the plan to the school calendar. For example, if one objective is to produce a year-by-year overview then having it ready for a department meeting makes good sense. The school calendar will hopefully indicate when department meetings will take place and so saying that it must be done by 2 June is a good thing as it means that the manager can keep track of the plan. Put simply, if the year-by-year overview isn't produced on 2 June then you can ask why, but also you know that the team's ability to deliver the plan is in doubt as an objective hasn't been met. On their own, missing deadlines may not be all that serious but the cumulative effect of missing several deadlines can lead to slippage on a grand scale.

The other reason for having this level of specificity is to see whether the plan is overambitious or underambitious for the team. It is very easy to get carried away in a team planning meeting and to set out to do too much. Thinking realistically about all the steps that need to be taken gives the team the opportunity to think about how it is going to divide up its work and the impact that this will have. Similarly, when you start to break a job down into its constituent parts then it may not appear as onerous as it first did. This may mean that you can programme further development, or move it to a time when things are not very busy.

Budget

Being a good manager includes being able to plan how the money you have been allowed will be spent. In addition, in the same senses as we argued at the beginning of the chapter, it is also very much about being able to demonstrate that the department offers value for money.

Responsibility and accountability

These are two different but linked aspects of management. The first is to say who is responsible for making sure that something happens – not necessarily doing it but making sure that it is done. The second concerns being accountable for an outcome.

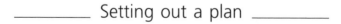

Setting out a plan

Your school might already have a format that it wants you to use for development planning purposes. The usual reason for this is harmonisation across the various teams and this aids the leadership team in whole-school planning and department monitoring. However, if you have the choice, or the influence, to do it another way then it is a useful discussion area as to what will enable the team to plan and monitor its work.

In the example part-plan in Table 7.2, we have tried to show how the different elements described can be made to fit together – French teachers may have other ideas about how such an aim can be realised!

Implementing the plan

The next stage, having planned out what the team is going to do, is to start to do it. Implementation is something that people can find difficult because it doesn't involve the highly creative work that putting a plan together does. The first stage is to provide everyone with a copy of the plan and to have a large scale reproduction of it displayed in the department base or office. This helps to remind people of what they are going to do, of the importance of the plan and, of course, that the time for planning is over – the time for implementation has begun.

Having a personal meeting with each member of the department to go through their individual contribution and role is good practice. If the department is large – for example a science department with a head of physics, chemistry and biology – then giving the postholders responsibility for organising individual meetings strengthens their role and their accountability to you.

Monitoring the implementation of the plan and collecting the information you need for self-evaluation

Monitoring the work of the team is one of the key responsibilities for the team leader and is absolutely essential for maintaining the momentum you create.

One way of increasing the scope of the monitoring and at the same time reduce it as a managerial task is to include the development plan as a regular item on team meetings. By creating an expectation among the team that it is their responsibility to present the outcomes of their development plan work at the meeting, the team itself becomes the monitoring medium.

Going back to the idea of the autonomous department, there is a need for the department to know itself and to be able to evaluate its own work in relation to student progress and development planning. To make self-evaluation a natural part of the team's activity, it is good practice to collect information as the year progresses.

TABLE 7.2 French improvement plan

Aim 1: To raise attainment of the most able students

Primary objective	Desired outcome	Required actions	Timescale	Budget source	Resp:	Acc to:
1.1 To have a well-planned curriculum that addresses the needs of the most able.	The curriculum for set 1 will be planned on a lesson-by-lesson basis and will include a wide range of extension material to ensure that the needs of the most able are met.	Write a curriculum statement that explains how the most able children progress in French – what do we want to observe at each key stage?	3 April	Staffing	A named person	Head of department
		Write a curriculum statement that identifies the progress that the most able need to make year-by-year in reading, writing, speaking and listening.	10 April	Staffing		Head of department
		Write a curriculum plan for each key stage.	20 April	Staffing		Head of department
		Carry out year-by-year overviews.	25 April	Staffing		Head of department
		Carry out term-by-term overviews.	3 May	Staffing		Head of department
		Agree templates for curriculum – year-by-year, term-by-term and lesson-by-lesson plans.	10 May	Staffing		Deputy head – quality of teaching
		Produce three summative assessments for each year at Key Stage 3 that will test the most able.	13 May	INSET – 4 hours		Deputy head – quality of learning

Action	Date	Resource	Responsible
Lessons planned on a lesson-by-lesson basis with learning outcomes for all of Key Stage 3 – Year 7 Term 1, Year 8 Term 1, Year 9 Term 1.	27 May	INSET – gained time	Head of department
Lessons planned on a lesson-by-lesson basis with learning outcomes for all of Key Stage 3 – Year 7 Term 2, Year 8 Term 2, Year 9 Term 2.	14 June	INSET – gained time	Head of department
Lessons planned on a lesson-by-lesson basis with learning outcomes for all of Key Stage 3 – Year 7 Term 3, Year 8 Term 3, Year 9 Term 3.	27 June	INSET – gained time	Head of department
Collate all the lesson plans into one folder and audit the programme.	1 July	Resources – £700	Head of department
Order the materials to support the teaching programme.	3 July	Textbooks, CD and DVD resources – £2750	Head of department
Produce the in-house materials.	9 July	Resources – £700	Head of department

TABLE 7.3   Collecting evidence for evaluation

Domain of evidence	Data source	To evaluate
Internally generated	Assessment – by creating some form of database the department can store all of the information from summative assessments.	Pupil progress.
	Attendance – at revision classes or extracurricular events.	How well the events match the interests and needs of students.
	Recruitment to courses.	How well the courses match the interests and needs of students.
	Lesson judgements.	Quality of teaching in the department.
	Department detentions and incident forms.	How well the department manages students.
Externally generated	Assessment – performance in key stage tests.	Pupil progress and the efficacy of internal assessments.
School generated	Teaching judgements.	The quality of teaching in the department and the efficacy of internal department monitoring.

The type of information collected will vary across departments but Table 7.3 exemplifies some domains of evidence.

The purpose in collecting the data is simple – it provides the evidence base for you to be able to answer the critical questions that form part of your self-evaluation.

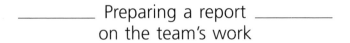

Preparing a report on the team's work

Writing a self-evaluation report on the department's work is the team's opportunity to look critically at itself and to examine how well it is doing. Use the OfSTED criteria to help you to comment on these areas.

- *Overall effectiveness* – this is an overall statement of how the department is doing. Is it a very effective department – one where children do very well indeed with low costs – or ineffective – where children underachieve?

- *Improvement since the last self-evaluation* – the issues that were raised when the department last evaluated itself (or there was an OFSTED inspection) and how you have addressed them. Remember that this is about the impact that your interventions have had rather than what you have done.

- *Capacity to improve* – are there particular issues in your team that are making it very difficult for you to progress further (there may be staff shortages)?

- *What the department should do further* – what do you need to do next, why have you decided to do this and how will you know if it has worked?

- *Achievement and standards* – how well are the students doing and are standards high?

- *Personal development* – how has the department made use of INSET to develop the capacity of the team?

- *Quality of provision* – taking into account the budget you have, your staff, your facilities, the course you offer, the resources you use and the results obtained, how would you summarise your department?

- *Leadership and management* – how do you assess your leadership and management of the department?

There are critical questions to answer as part of self-evaluation. Looking closely at the development plan and assessing the impact of the activity is the first stage of this. Above all, you are aiming to answer the following questions.

- How well is the department doing?

- What does it need to do to improve?

- How do you know that is where the weaknesses lie?

- How will you know that the improvement has been made?

Summary

Planning the work of the department and monitoring its path to improvement is an increasingly important aspect of the team leader's role as schools become more autonomous. In this chapter we have discussed how the concept of the autonomous school can be applied to the department.

The critical issues for the middle manager are that the department should be in a position to plan its own work on the basis of its own self-evaluation. It should know itself well and be able to assess its own progress, as well as that of others.

Moving on, moving forward

– the importance of professional development

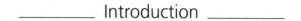 Introduction

In this chapter we look at professional development for the middle manager. Earlier in the book we discussed the opportunities for professional development that would help you to secure a middle management role. Here we show why it is important to carry on developing and look at the various opportunities available to grow as a professional. For some people, taking on the role of head of department will be the stepping stone to a career in school leadership (at deputy head or headteacher level) but for others it will represent their ambition fulfilled. Whatever the long-term range of your career it is important to think most about what you are doing now – have your eye on what you might like to do in the future but the focus has to be what you are going to do in the time you spend as a middle manager. Being in this role gives you the opportunity to develop an understanding of what leadership and management mean in the context of a school. We will also be examining some ideas of organisational theory to underpin the discussion.

Professional development

When David Hopkins gave a presentation to the SSAT (Specialist Schools and Academies Trust) 13th National Conference (2005) he called his thesis *System Leadership and School Transformation*. In his speech he talked about the drivers for educational transformation – one of these is the need for a professionalisation of teaching. The slide he presented is reproduced in Figure 8.1.

In some ways this illustrates the need for professional development. There is no longer one way that teachers are trained, there is no longer one way of teaching – if ever the latter were the case. There are a number of routes into teaching – the traditional PGCE, the GRTP (Graduate Recruitment Trainee Programme), SCITT (School-based Initial Teacher Training), the B.Ed and there will be others to come for sure. Many heads of department and middle managers have responsibility for managing students from university departments and others following the range of routes into teaching. Put simply, these people bring a new, non-traditional approach to teacher training and their needs are diverse – they will demand a mentor who has a different approach to their education. The impact of National Strategies and other programmes is such that a broader range of approaches to pedagogy and practice has developed. The way in which

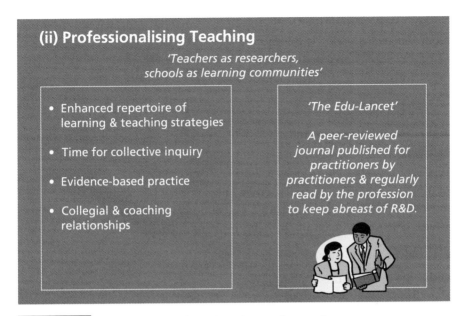

(ii) Professionalising Teaching

'Teachers as researchers,
schools as learning communities'

- Enhanced repertoire of learning & teaching strategies
- Time for collective inquiry
- Evidence-based practice
- Collegial & coaching relationships

'The Edu-Lancet'

A peer-reviewed journal published for practitioners by practitioners & regularly read by the profession to keep abreast of R&D.

FIG. 8.1 Drivers for educational transformation

teachers are trained varies considerably and there is an increasing emphasis on the craft of teaching. As Hopkins illustrates in the above slide, as teaching enters the next phase it will be dominated by those who are ready to reassert the role of the teacher in formulating strategy. The relationship between academics and practice in school is really to the fore. The work of Wiliam and Black in developing *Assessment for Learning* was carried out in the Institute of Education but was developed in schools; the 'nine gateways' to personalised learning set out by David Hargreaves as part of a collaboration between the SSAT and SHA (now ASCL) has been promulgated through the work in schools – see the pamphlets written by Hargreaves – for example Personalising Learning–2 (2004). There is a real need for teachers to develop their repertoires to take the best from the proliferation of practice developments – and, indeed, to personalise it for themselves as they seek to personalise the learning experience for the children in their classes. A critical dimension of this new era of educational debate is that the answers do not lie in the minds of others – the 'they' that have persisted in informing teachers what they should and should not do, but more in the 'us' and 'you' in the sense that everyone has a shared collective responsibility for professional development to inform how the debate is shaped in the future.

There is perhaps a more pragmatic reason why professional development matters. In March 2004 there was a report in the 7 March edition of the *Sunday Times* entitled *A third of Britons are bored at work*. Development Dimensions International interviewed 1000 staff from companies employing more than 500 workers for its spring research report. Many were bored, lacking commitment and ready to quit. They did not believe that their employers would try to get them to stay if they resigned. The managing director of DDI said 'the data show that anywhere between 10% and 33% of the workforce are so disengaged that it has to have a significant impact on productivity. They bring only 50% of themselves to work when they come through the door in the morning'. Later in the article, a list was given of the reasons why people leave their jobs:

- better promotion chances
- the desire for more challenging work
- a more exciting place to work
- more varied work
- pay.

This research wasn't about teaching but it is worth thinking about it in the context of professional development. Pay comes a long way down the list and some of the above are beyond the scope and power of a middle manager – but the need to provide people with challenging stimulating work is clear. The survey found that employees who do not get helpful feedback on their performance are twice as likely to lack commitment to their organisation. Clearly, the middle manager should have this in their scope to ensure that the team receive helpful feedback and that their work is stimulating and challenging. Of course, the middle manager is managed as well – therefore, the question can be asked, how do you ensure that you get what you give to others. One aspect of human interaction is that if you cannot provide a challenging environment for others then it is not a challenging environment for you too – the nature of interaction will ensure that the level of challenge you provide for others will be reciprocated. Stopping others from getting bored starts with stopping yourself from getting bored.

There has been a paradigm shift in the nature of school management and leadership over the past few years and it is with this in mind that we consider how to ensure that your career stays on track. Handy (1995) records how, in the newer, more hi-tech organisations in the USA, the word 'manager' had begun to disappear. People ceased to be described as managers and were identified as 'team leaders', 'project leaders', 'co-ordinators' or, more generally, 'executives'. The language is significant because it signals a change in attitude and, perhaps, a new way of looking at the world. The implication behind the word 'manager' is that there are people to be managed in a stratified society.

Management

A further implication of this cultural shift is that management ceases to be a definition of status and becomes an activity. As such it can be defined and the associated skills taught, learnt and developed. Handy (1995) describes the position in the late 1980s as the 'hangover of management as a class' and the amateur status of British managers in comparison with those in other countries. It is in this context that educational management needs to be seen. Educational management is, according to Glatter (1979), concerned with the 'internal operation of educational institutions, and also with their relationships with their environments'. School leaders play a key role in formulating the aims or goals of the institution. They have a particular responsibility for establishing and maintaining an effective management structure. These managerial functions might be regarded as essentially practical activities – setting goals, making decisions and building relationships involve action. This, in part, explains the plethora of management courses which have been considered vital for any career teacher's professional development.

Some practitioners, however, have been dismissive of theories and concepts because they are thought to be remote from the realities of schools and classrooms. Bush (1989) describes a scenario where a manager takes a decision. In deciding on the most appropriate response to a particular problem, the manager draws on a range of options suggested by previous encounters with this type of issue. If pressed to explain the reasons for the decision, the practitioner is likely to say that it is simply 'common sense'. However, this is often based on an implicit theory of the best way to deal with the situation. In a sense, theorising takes place without it being acknowledged as such. Bush argues, however, that those managers who operate on the basis of an unrecognised theory tend to have a one-dimensional outlook on organisational life simply as a consequence of being wedded to a single, narrow perspective.

This is not to argue that theory is more important than practice. Theory provides a rationale for decision making. It helps managers by giving them a basis for action. An appreciation of theory may also reduce the time required to achieve managerial effectiveness by compensating for a lack of certain levels of experience. This is how the middle manager moves from being a teacher to being an effective manager and leader.

Organisational theory

There has been a shift from management to leadership; there is also a sea change in the nature of organisational theory. Before considering the way in which successful schools operate it is necessary to consider the bureaucratic model of school management articulated by Weber (1947). In a complicated article, Weber describes the nature of legal authority in an organisation. For Weber, a person in authority occupies an 'office'. In the actions associated with his/her status, including the commands he/she issues to others, the officeholder is subject to an impersonal order to which his/her actions are oriented. In this sense, the person who obeys authority does so in his/her capacity as a member of the corporate group over whom the authority is exercised – his/her obedience is to the impersonal order.

It is worthwhile considering this model further. The organisation of these offices follows the principle of hierarchy – the lower office is under the control and supervision of the higher one. The rules which regulate the conduct of an office may be technical rules or norms. In both cases, if their application is to be fully rational then specialised training is necessary. Weber identifies particular features which are pertinent to this consideration of the school as an organisation:

- teachers are organised in a clearly defined hierarchy of offices
- each office has a clearly defined sphere of competence, in the legal sense
- candidates are selected on the basis of technical qualifications – they are appointed
- teachers are remunerated by fixed salaries in money – the salary scales are primarily graded according to rank in the hierarchy; but in addition to this criterion, the responsibility of the position may be taken into account
- it constitutes a career – promotion is dependent on the judgement of superiors.

Before we leave this analysis of the hierarchical model of school leadership it is useful to reflect on the ways in which schools in the twenty-first century still operate this paradigm. If we think about the head of subject, there are three activities in particular that embody Weber's analysis of bureaucracy. The first is the purchasing power of the head of subject – they usually have purchasing authority for the resources that the department needs. The authority derives from their core purpose – to manage the subject. Secondly, the head of subject is responsible for developing the programmes of study because it is within the subject leader's sphere of competence. Lastly, the core purpose of the subject leader is to provide professional leadership for a subject to secure high-quality teaching, effective use of resources and improved standards of learning for all pupils (see Chapter 2). This is an example of the clearly defined hierarchy of the office.

The importance of this theoretical perspective lies in the framework that it gives to our understanding of how schools work as organisations. If you are to progress you need some understanding of the nature of a school as an organisation.

Weber provided the dominant theoretical perspective on organisations as bureaucracies. Despite the pervasive influence of Weber's work there have been few attempts to document applications of his theory to British education. One exception is the article by Harling (1984 in Bush, ed. (1989)) – this is useful further reading. The strength of this article lies in Harling's analysis of the complexity of the educational system. The educational system as a whole is 'an organisation' and yet it possesses constituent 'organisations' at various levels. An organisation is one which exists and is formally established for the explicit purpose of achieving certain goals. In a bureaucracy, subunits are clearly subordinate to the central leadership and are expected to accept, and work towards achieving, the goals set by the leaders. In a collegium it is assumed that members agree about the objectives of the institution because these are largely based on shared values. It depends on an initial agreement about aims. The notion of a collegial body as an educational institution, derived from the essential difference between it and many other organisations, is that schools have large numbers of professional staff. Moreover, these professionals have substantial discretion in performing their teaching role. The effective management of schools depends on the cooperation of the professionals – or, at a minimum, their acquiescence.

A key element to the collegial perspective is the professional competence of the teachers. In its purest form, all members of the collegium have an equal opportunity to influence policies. Noble and Pym (in Bush, ed. (1989)) discuss some of the difficulties that can arise when the collegial approach is accompanied by an elaborate system of committees. The adoption of collegial approaches has been particularly evident in primary schools where teachers are assumed to have a responsibility for one element of the curriculum as well as for teaching their own class.

An understanding of these issues is necessary before you can focus your attention on the moves you intend to make.

TASK 22

Decision making at your school

Think about your own school, or the school you would like to work at, and consider these questions.

- At what level are the aims of the school decided and how are they decided?

- How are decisions made at the school?

- How would you describe the organisational structure?

- Are there links between the school and the external environment?

- How would you describe the leadership of the school?

In response to these questions, Table 8.1 compares the two organisational perspectives.

The value in considering these perspectives is that they give us useful and valid insight into the nature of management. They represent different ways of analysing educational institutions. The applicability of each

TABLE 8.1 Comparing organisational perspectives

Question	Bureaucratic perspective	Collegial perspective
At what level are the aims of the school decided and how are they decided?	Aims are determined by the headteacher and perhaps the leadership team.	There are policy groups which consider questions and create shared objectives.
How are decisions made at the school?	Decisions are based on objectives. There is an analysis of issues and decisions are taken in line with the hierarchical structure.	Decisions are characterised by thorough discussion of proposals and collaboration.

TABLE 8.1 *(cont'd)*

Question	Bureaucratic perspective	Collegial perspective
How would you describe the organisational structure?	Decisions move from top to bottom. There are rigid job descriptions which are expressed in terms of production, evaluation, checking, reporting etc. There is a sense in which collaboration develops from the structure.	Areas may be specified but are often negotiated and draw on strengths and expertise. The structure develops from the collaboration.
Are there links between the school and the external environment?	Parents will go through an established procedure. The headteacher reports to the governors.	Links with other schools are created and sustained through networks. Typically each teacher has authority to contact parents.
How would you describe the leadership of the school?	This is characterised by didactic, rigid, consultative, deterministic leadership management.	This is characterised by cooperation, empathy, discursive management.

model depends on the nature of the organisation and the event or situation under consideration.

In recent years there has been a movement towards a fuller consideration of the nature of school leadership and from this has developed a concept whereby teachers and students become integrated into the process of leading a school. From this have emerged two fundamental processes – the exercise of leadership and the practice of teaching and learning. For years, those running the system – headteachers, teachers and school governors – knew nothing of research into school effectiveness and school improvement.

Brighouse and Woods (1989) describe the seven processes which encompass most activities in school life (see Table 8.2).

Thinking about how you operate – and how decisions are made in your school and in your department or team – is vital if you are to maximise the effectiveness of what you do to build an inclusive team. This applies at whatever level you are in the school.

TABLE 8.2   Brighouse and Woods' seven processes

- The practice of teaching and learning.
- The exercise of leadership.
- The practice of management and organisation.
- The practice of collective review.
- The creation of an environment most suitable for learning.
- The promotion of staff development.
- The encouragement of parental and community involvement.

Teachers as learners

Improving schools are learning organisations – this theme has been discussed several times in this book. Teachers teach, but they also need to be advanced learners in order to develop new skills and insights. Teachers need to keep up to date with their area of expertise and with recent research about pedagogy. They have to keep up to date with legislative changes that affect their work, such as the national curriculum, assessment, inspection and appraisal. Learning needs to be continuous in order to enable teachers to improve classroom practice, contribute to whole-school issues, manage change and acquire new skills.

MacGilchrist, Myers and Reed (1997) discuss motivation in teacher learning. There have been surveys of teacher morale – the long-term effect of being told that what is done is inadequate and references to the numbers of incompetent teachers are not conducive to high levels of morale. However, the literature on school improvement (reviewed in MacGilchrist et al.) suggests that teachers need to find both meaning and 'ownership' in order to want to participate in change efforts. As the future leaders of schools – whether at middle or senior level – teachers need to acknowledge the ways in which they can motivate their colleagues most effectively. As a leader, a teacher can be the one who provides the opportunities for learning to be put to good use, and for maximising student progress and achievement.

In seeking to make the transition from middle manager to senior manager, the teacher needs to consider the range of experiences that will be necessary for such a role.

The most important feature in a teacher's portfolio of experience is that of excellence in the classroom and a record, over time, of successful teaching. To this end it is essential to keep records of the classes taught and the results obtained. This, of course, is required for threshold assessment.

The move to a more senior role is characterised by the nature of the job itself. As a senior manager, the responsibility lies not with a team of staff (e.g. a subject team, a year team etc.) but with whole-school issues. The middle manager needs to get experience of involvement in and the leadership of initiatives that address whole-school issues. Further, there is a range of tasks typically associated with senior management of which the middle manager can gain some experience.

We think it is important that if you decide to get involved in activities outside your department or team role then they should be seen as part of your ongoing professional development rate rather than just being like 'Brownie badges' that you acquire on the path to your next role. Although there is a certain amount of pragmatism in selecting which projects you get involved with, selecting only those that add to your CV can cause resentment and might mean that you miss out on other opportunities. Getting involved is a professional requirement for wider effectiveness (in the way envisaged and expected in threshold standards). The following is an extract from the Teachers Pay and Conditions Document (2005).

Wider professional effectiveness

6 Teachers should demonstrate that they take responsibility for their professional development and use the outcomes to improve their teaching and pupils' learning.

7 Teachers should demonstrate that they make an active contribution to the policies and aspirations of the school.

Professional characteristics

8 Teachers should demonstrate that they are effective professionals who challenge and support all pupils to do their best through:

(a) inspiring trust and confidence

(b) building team commitment

(c) engaging and motivating pupils

(d) analytical thinking

(e) positive action to improve the quality of pupils' learning.

There is a clear imperative for this involvement both as part of the job and as part of gaining the necessary skills and experiences for the future.

There is a range of activities that might lie outside the scope of what middle managers might normally become involved in. We discuss each of these briefly, considering what might be learnt from participating in these school-wide projects.

Projects to develop skills and experiences for leadership team roles:

- *Timetabling and curriculum planning* – this is one of the major planning tasks that is undertaken in a school and involvement is a good opportunity to learn a whole range of skills. The importance of the school timetable as a curriculum planning tool and organisational management device cannot be overstated. Think about how you feel when you first see your timetable – when you look in horror when you realise that your least favourite class have a double lesson with you on Friday afternoon! The timetable is about the experience of children – how their day is structured – and also about how the staff are deployed and how the premises are used throughout the day. A good timetable includes a well-constructed pupil day and manageable staff deployment undertaken at cost. When you add into the timetable the link with homework timetables then the impact of the timetable as an organisational tool becomes apparent. Different schools have different ways of managing the construction of the timetable – it is often led by a member of the leadership team and this provides you with the opportunity to work alongside an experienced school leader. The pressure to complete the timetable can be considerable and as such requires a huge amount of work during a very short time – but it is time limited as a consequence.

- *Working groups* – on curriculum planning and other areas of teaching and learning. From time to time schools review their curricula and consider how their assessment policies and practices are working. Getting involved in working groups should be seen as part of your job, but positioning yourself to lead such a working group is a good experience. The experience of leading a group will give you an opportunity to work with a range of people and to have your thinking challenged. It will also give you the opportunity to hone your skills when responding to the differing views of others. Finally, it will enable you to develop organisational skills as you arrange topics for discussion, report back to the leadership team (or other sponsor) on progress and present your final outcomes.

- *Organising trips, visits* and *extracurricular activities* – responsibility for children, staff and money are three areas that can be fraught – mainly because if things go wrong then the consequences can be catastrophic.

Making arrangements to take a group of people on a trip gives you the opportunity to practise risk assessment skills, organise itineraries, manage large sums of money and exercise the absolute responsibility that only comes from looking after other people's children.

■ *Working with governors* – this is a very important area and few get the opportunity to learn about how the governing body works and its relationship with the school. Governing bodies vary considerably – some will have associate governors, who can be part of the structure but cannot vote on certain topics, including pupil discipline and the budget for example. The most straightforward route is to be elected as teacher governor. This will involve you being a teacher governor for four years – this is statutory. Most governing bodies organise themselves into committees to cover finance, personnel, premises and curriculum. Being a teacher governor is not the same as being a teacher union representative where you are representing a union – you are a teacher governor by virtue of your status as a teacher of the school. By being a teacher governor you will have access to much information about how the school is run and organised – how the school budget is drawn up, policies developed etc.

Whatever projects you decide to involve yourself in, it is important that you do a really good job and that you don't let this external work affect the way in which you carry out your main role. By maximising these opportunities you gain the experience of a wider group of people, as well as being exposed to a greater range of issues and variety of opinions.

Courses for teacher learners

In Chapter 4 we discussed a range of professional development opportunities offered by SSAT and NCSL, to name but two. There is a range of courses and we discuss several of them in this section.

'Leading from the middle'

The National College for School Leadership offers a course called *Leading from the Middle*. This is a 10-month professional development programme for groups of two to four middle leaders in primary, secondary and special schools. There are opportunities for applications from single schools or from groups of schools working together as a collaborative. This course is organised and administered by the NCSL and focuses on five key areas:

- leadership of innovation and change
- knowledge and understanding of an individual's role in leading teaching and learning
- enhancing self-confidence and skills as team leaders
- building team capacity through the efficient use of staff and resources
- active engagement in self-directed change in a blended learning environment.

As a programme, it seeks to make itself relevant to a wide range of practitioners in subject-based and pastoral roles and with different levels of experience. The online materials and the experience of tutors reflect this variation. The NCSL recommends that participants have at least two years' experience in a middle leader role in order to gain maximum benefit from the self-reflection elements of the programme. Participants are formed into small groups and each group of two to four middle leaders is supported by a leadership coach. The leadership coach is usually a more experienced leader based in the same school and acts in a supporting/mentoring role throughout the programme.

Leadership and professional development programmes by SSAT

SSAT runs a range of programmes including the developing leaders programmes and others to develop leadership in specialism areas. This is an example of the programme for the *Director of Specialism* course.
  Objectives:

- To gain a better understanding of the chosen specialist status.
- To become more effective in leading and managing the specialism plan.
- To gain insight into ways of meeting the targets from other practitioners.
- To update on new curriculum and pedagogy in the chosen specialism.
- To set up and sustain a network with other directors of specialism.
- To share innovative practice.

A typical organisation for such a course follows.

Day 1 – School-based workshop

On registration some materials will be available for preparation and planning for the first day.

After each session there will be a reflection on points learnt and possible actions needed when returning to school. At the end of day one there will be an opportunity to reflect and develop your action plan.

9.00   Registration and coffee

9.20   *Programme overview*
- Introduction and clarifying objectives.
- Introduction of the action plan.

9.40   *What is the role of a director of specialism*
- What is the role and how does it fit into management?
- Host school explaining the role of their director of specialism.
- Record points in action plan.

10.15   *Specialism overview*
- The big picture
- Redesignation issues
- What does being a specialist school mean and why?

10.45   *Evaluation and monitoring of specialist school status*
- Evaluating the position of your school using the monitoring tool provided.
- Working in pairs to discuss school and community plans.
- Discussion about issues arising.
- Record points in action plan.

11.30   Coffee

11.45   *How do I deliver the key targets*?
- The use of data to track progress.
- Ideas on data management tools.
- Examples of good practice from the host school.
- Illustrations of how these relate to your specialism and your role of director of specialism.
- Record points in action plan.

Lunch   *What does a specialist school look like*?

1.00
- Tour of host school during lunch.
- Possible interactive presentation showing examples of pupils' work.

1.50   *What does innovation look like for my specialism*?
- Innovation in your specialism.
- Sharing good practice.
- Specialism specific issues.
- Record points in action plan.

3.10 *Making the plan work*
- Know your team and appropriate intervention strategies.
- Action planning and risk assessment.
- Record points in action plan.

3.45 *The way forward*
- Personal evaluation and ways forward on return to school.
- Review and develop action plan.
- Contact details given of your e-mentor.

4.15 Departure and coffee

Implementing your action plan

- Throughout the following term you will implement your action plan from the workshop (Day 1).
- Help will be available throughout this term from your e-mentor – providing telephone and e-mail support.
- Support and networking from your group is available through an e-forum.
- Your e-mentor will contact you within a week with ideas for a learning journey outlined with options – for example, suggestions of resources available, focused reading list, examples of good practice, case studies, use of lead practitioners and other possible professional development opportunities.
- You will provide feedback, on Day 2, of your progress – including successes and failures!

Day 2 – **School-based workshop**

9.00 Registration and coffee

9.20 *Introduction*

9.30 *Your action plan feedback*
- Delegates present their feedback from implementing their action plan.
- Follow-up on analysis of school results and issues arising from use of the monitoring and evaluation tools, to include in-depth discussion that is specialism-specific.

11.30 Coffee

11.45 *How do I get the whole school and community involved?*
- Cross-curricular working.
- Introducing a specialism ethos.
- Enrichment activities.
- Examples of good community involvement.

Lunch *What does specialist education look like to a student?*
1.00 ■ Listening to the student voice.
      ■ Opportunities to talk to students about learning in a specialist environment.
      ■ Exploring their work.

1.50 *What does 'vocational' and '14–19' mean to your school?*

2.35 *New technologies and how you can use them.*

3.10 *Gifted and talented – sharing good practice.*

3.45 *What next for you?*
      ■ Other professional development opportunities.
      ■ Working towards a Masters qualification.
      ■ Maintaining your action plan.
      ■ Further help and resources.

4.15 Departure and coffee

The benefit of being involved in programmes such as this is that it gives you the opportunity to work with leading practitioners. SSAT offers programmes that are 'for schools, by schools' and so the currency and credibility is high.

Higher degrees and research

As an individual, you may have a need to find out the information – or find the knowledge or expertise possessed by a colleague. The importance of management courses, such as the MA degree, is emphasised by the need for organisations to continue along the road of self-review and continuous improvement.

The *Study Guide* to the Open University's MA course *Educational Management in Action* sets out clearly the reasons why an aspirant middle manager should consider further study. The *Study Guide* states the aims of the course as:

. . . to develop your skills of investigation and reflection in order to improve your own management practice and assist others to improve theirs.

This statement emphasises our assertion that the motivation for such a course of study should be about improving one's professional practice. This is achieved through developing a theoretical basis for the management practices that are developed. Further, the need for reflection is stressed – the leader and manager of the future needs to be someone who can research a problem and, when a solution is proposed, can reflect on the strategy and the practices involved. This is the virtue of such courses – the opportunity to develop an in-depth understanding and to articulate theories on leadership and management is essential training for the practitioner.

Some people will baulk at the idea of lots of bookwork and essay writing. The choice of the most appropriate course is key. Most Masters courses have a taught element assessed through coursework assignments, examinations and dissertations. Some courses, however, are structured to accommodate the needs of the modern schoolteacher – managers often want a report on an issue, rather than an essay. Therefore, courses such as the OU MA have incorporated this into the assessment process – there is an emphasis on reflective practice, action research and management style reports.

There are many different courses available. A popular one is the SSAT *Developing Leaders* course. This has several elements including an international link, the opportunity to attend the national conference and to do a number of assignments that can be used as part of a certificated course with a points value towards an MA. Universities are wise to the fact that people want flexibility in their study and so there is a 'portable' quality to many courses. Again, this means that courses have a points value – a year-long course at Masters level will normally be worth 60 points; 180 are needed for the award of an MA. Also, if you study one course at one institution, a second course with a different institution, then the third course can be studied at yet another institution before the qualification is awarded. The compatibility issue is important and guidance is offered by universities on this. It is really important to keep good records of study because the original transcripts of academic records are normally required before the study is validated.

The programme offered by SSAT has the following aims and objectives.

Overarching aims

- To provide succession planning for specialist schools at a time when demographic trends indicate a growing shortage of school leaders.

- To provide high quality, practitioner-led professional development experiences for all participants.

- To contribute to the transformation of the secondary school workforce and raise achievement by developing future school leaders.

Developing Leaders for Tomorrow – course aims

- Acquire skills, knowledge and insights from good practice exhibited in high performing, innovative specialist schools.

- Gain national and international perspective, and understanding of key issues affecting school performance.

- Develop critical and analytical skills using first-hand observation, and a case study to examine the characteristics of successful innovative practices in specialist schools.

- Provide an opportunity for teachers at an early stage in their careers to understand school structures, systems and strategies for the management of change.

- For participants who complete the course, to gain either a Specialist Schools Trust Diploma or a Post-Graduate Certificate in Innovation in Education.

Developing Leaders for Tomorrow – course objectives

- To establish and develop networks in order to share knowledge.

- To participate in a project linked to a partner school that raises achievement and transforms learning.

- To develop an understanding of leadership skills in a business setting.

- To develop international links and an international perspective to research.

- To take part in an international study tour (optional).

Developing Leaders for Tomorrow – learning outcomes

- A theoretical knowledge and practical awareness of the elements that constitute school design – including organisation of physical space – the psychology of learning, curriculum design and scheduling – including personalisation of the curriculum.

- Knowledge of the principles that underpin innovation in a school context.

- Understanding of the link between innovation and school improvement.

- Knowledge of the theory of successful leadership and its application to the school context.

- Understanding of the link between successful leadership and school improvement.

One of the benefits of extended study is a greater understanding of the issues that face managers and this is the basis for improving practice. What enables the teacher to move into management is an understanding of the need for management and the principles of management. When considering the move to middle management, the individual has to consider what kind of model they will embody. What will be the principles on which they will act? To do this, there has to come first an understanding of the issues of school management and leadership.

The idea of learning management theory is attractive to some people in its own right. However, for the majority there needs to be a point to the task. Doing further study is hard work – coming home after a day's teaching to the prospect of three hours' academic study is quite a daunting prospect. However, if the aim of the course is to improve one's ability to apply knowledge of educational management to daily life and to reflect on this knowledge then the task becomes easier.

However, the prospect of further study needs to be considered carefully. While the outcome is desirable – in that it increases management potential and prepares one for more senior positions – the prospect of the work is not always so attractive. There are a number of issues to consider:

- support from school
- support from home
- financial implications
- managing the time.

The benefits of further study should not just be confined to the individual. If you want to embark on a course of study that is designed to improve your professional practice then it is proper to discuss this with a member of the senior team. Often, they will have done further study themselves and so will be aware of the task being undertaken. Engaging their support is important because if there is a need for additional information then early discussion will help to ease the way. Also, if the school can foresee a benefit then there are ways in which it can provide support in the form of timetabling – perhaps blocking time for the teacher to study – mentoring and possibly helping with negotiations with other staff. In some cases, there may be financial assistance for the cost of fees.

Professional development through research

As a middle manager, there is a need to reflect on the nature of subject knowledge and how it impacts on the development of teaching excellence. A key feature of educational research over recent years has been the involvement of teachers. While there have always been opportunities for teachers to engage in research as part of diploma and higher degree courses, Information and Communication Technology makes the involvement of a wider range of teachers possible. However, the nature of educational research has changed. The earlier articles to which we have referred focused on the seminal and universal aspects of research. However, the practice of ethnographic research has illustrated the difficulty in constructing theory based on one study – it is a body of knowledge.

What is the future for educational research and how can middle managers develop this as part of their professional development? At a conference in March 2000, Professor Pring (University of Oxford, Department of Educational Studies) asked the question 'How can research be useful?' The context of the recent debate has been about developing teaching as a research or evidence-based profession. Traditionally, the model has been one in which universities carry out research and relevant findings are then applied to schools. There has been widespread criticism of research, particularly in the Hillage report (1998). Some of the criticisms that have been levelled are that research is fragmented, inaccessible to practitioners, written by and for academics, published in journals that few read and, above all, it does not answer the questions of interest to practitioners.

A key development has been the comparison with advances in the medical field. Here there is a similar emphasis on evidence-based practice. The Cochrane Centre sets out to provide extensive reviews of all research evidence in a particular medical field. Medical practitioners and researchers work together to identify the issues to be reviewed. The outcomes of the reviews are intended to provide evidence to assist in the making of professional judgements – not to provide prescriptions for practice.

An approach like this offers two significant potential benefits. The first is that engaging in research enterprises could be a key source of professional satisfaction and could enhance the standing of those involved in education. The other is that it could result in the bringing together of interested individuals and institutions into professional communities.

Fortunately the broad range of courses available to teachers that incorporate a research element have moved things on considerably – it is not uncommon for courses to undertake small- to large-scale research projects and to report the outcomes in journals and periodicals.

It is essential that one's partner is aware of the implications before the course begins. In taking on additional work, there is a clear need for time to be spent. This may be at the expense of caring for children or attending to the myriad of domestic responsibilities that need looking after. Also, if there is no financial support from the school there are fees to be paid and the course to be resourced. These matters need to be discussed and planned.

The benefits of professional study are immense and are not confined to those explored above. By planning a course of study which involves researching an issue, one becomes adept at managing one's time. Having to consider a range of tasks – preparing for lessons, marking books, reading a book on management, having a relationship – is part of the modern teacher's life. The opportunity to develop time management strategies is a lesson well learnt and one which stands us in good stead as we progress.

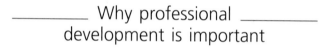

Why professional development is important

Professional development is a must – it is something that, as a leader, you have a responsibility to undertake. At its most fundamental it is part of the conditions of service for a teacher, but it is also the means of growing as a professional teacher. In the government's *Five Year Strategy for Children and Learners* (July 2004 ref: cm6272) the imperative for professional development was emphasised.

Better teaching through investing in the workforce

35 Central to improvements in teaching and learning is excellent professional development for all teachers – with more emphasis on classroom observation, practice, training, coaching and mentoring. To build up teachers' demand for high quality training, and encourage them to drive their own development, we will refocus teacher appraisals to become teaching and learning reviews. These will ensure teachers are:

- focused on effective classroom practice, using assessment for learning effectively and using a range of teaching styles and strategies appropriately to promote personalised learning

- involved in the professional development that best matches the needs identified by the reviews; and are also offering coaching and mentoring to other teachers where they have the teaching and subject skills from which other teachers can benefit

- rewarded, and make progress in their careers, in ways that fairly reflect their classroom expertise and commitment to their continuing professional development.

It will not be enough to join the profession and then stop learning – if only to secure pay awards as the *Five Year Strategy* makes clear:

For senior teachers, pay progression on the upper pay scale will depend on demonstrating that they have both developed themselves professionally, and that they are providing regular coaching and mentoring to less expert teachers.

Summary

Managing people is a skill-based activity – the route is to have a range of opportunities that enable you to develop the skills to be able to manage. One of the most critical skills is the ability to reflect on what you have done, and also to think carefully about others' actions and outcomes. Moving from being able to organise to having the capacity to look at what has been achieved and the reasons for the success and failures is how we move into a leadership mode.

As teachers we have a clear responsibility for children's learning and there is an imperative for us to continue our own learning through professional development. At its simplest it is about trying things out – talking to others about what we are doing and engaging with others. That commitment to personal and professional growth is something that we can all do, whatever our circumstances.

References

Black, P. and Wiliam, D. (1999) 'Assessment for learning: beyond the black box', University of Cambridge School of Education.
Brighouse, T. and Woods, D. (1989) *How to Improve your School*, London: Routledge.
Bush, T. (1989) 'The nature of theory in educational management', *Managing Education: Theory and Practice*, ed. Bush, T. (1992), Buckingham: Open University Press.

Glatter, R. (1979) 'The nature of theory in educational management', *Managing Education: Theory and Practice*, ed. Bush, T. (1992), Buckingham: Open University Press.

Handy, C. (1995) *The Age of Unreason*, London: Arrow Books Ltd.

Hargreaves, D. (2004) *Personalised Learning 2 – Student Voice and Assessment for Learning*, ISBN 1-905150-03-02, SSAT.

Harling, P. (1984) 'The organizational framework for educational leadership', *Managing Education: Theory and Practice*, ed. Bush, T. (1992), Buckingham: Open University Press.

Hillage Report (1998) for the Department for Education and Employment.

MalGilchrist, B., Myers, K. and Reed, J. (1997) *The Intelligent School*, London: Paul Chapman Publishing Ltd.

Pring, R. (2000) 'Educational research: working together', *Continuing Professional Development Conference, March 2000*, University of Oxford Conference Notes.

Weber, M. (1947) 'Legal authority in a bureaucracy', *Managing Education: Theory and Practice*, ed. Bush, T. (1992), Buckingham: Open University Press.

chapter nine

Hard work and fun

– how to create the balance

Introduction

Practical tips

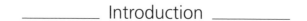

Introduction

This chapter isn't an advocacy of the five-mile run, or even about going to the gym on a regular basis, but it is about how to enjoy being a manager and how to create a balance. Is it the case that if you don't have the energy you haven't got a hope? Certainly, working in a school is demanding physically and mentally. The challenge of making learning fun while managing the high levels of progress that you want for the children in your classes makes for very full days and a high level of commitment. But it doesn't have to be exhausting and it doesn't have to be all encompassing to the exclusion of everything else. Working in a school is very rewarding – but it can be very challenging as well. Keeping it in perspective and learning some of the tricks of the trade is the theme of this final chapter.

Practical tips

Developing good practice and good habits helps to meet the challenge.

- *Keep a tidy classroom* – by having a tidy classroom you will make it easier for it to be cleaned and your working environment will be more pleasant. Some people like to have flowers in their classroom, photographs of their children or of their family on holiday – the point is that it is your working environment and it should be a place where you are comfortable, but also be a professional working environment. If there is clutter then the important thing is to get rid of it. It is difficult when you start in a new role to decide what to keep and what to discard, but if after a year you haven't used some materials then it is unlikely that you ever will. Having a major clear-out is cathartic and also enables you to find things quickly. Having a clean tidy working environment sends out important messages to staff and pupils – this is the standard that you expect from all.

- *Know the pupils* – this is a challenge, particularly when you move from one school to another. But it is essential if you are to be successful. It is important that you use the early months to meet pupils from other classes – perhaps through lesson observation or work scrutiny or surveys when seeking their views. By being a regular visitor to their classroom, you will be able to get to know the pupils as they are being taught in the department – and it means that when there is success or difficulty, you start from a position of strength because you know the pupil.

- *Make sure that pupils' work is celebrated* – this isn't about putting up displays. It is about making sure that pupils' work is displayed. Under workforce reform agreements you should not be putting up work for display personally but you are responsible for making sure that it happens. Secondary schools can be very bad places for displays but using the schemes of work to programme the production of display material you make it easier for people by making it systematic. The other aspect is that of rewards – as a subject leader or pastoral team leader you will frequently have to speak to pupils when they have done something wrong. Setting up systems where pupils are rewarded – perhaps with department certificates or letters home – is a positive way to get to know the students.

- *Be consistent* – when you have agreed a department or team policy it is important that everyone sticks to it. An effective way to manage the department is to agree a set of procedures – for example managing pupils in the corridor, frequency of marking, how textbooks are distributed and recorded, how orders are generated etc. If things aren't going well this enables you to be able to support staff from a position of strength. However, as well as supporting them through department policy there is an expectation that agreed standards will be upheld. So, if you have all agreed to file worksheets in the faculty office and someone doesn't then you will need to discuss that with that person.

- *Keep up the marking and assessment* – managing a large team does take extra effort and commitment, particularly in the early months. Keeping up with this is vital because you may have to discuss these matters with others, and therefore you have to make sure that you are leading by example. Asking colleagues for a sample of their marking is a reasonable request but discuss this so that it is agreed policy before you do it.

- *Keep up with the administration* – you can expect to get a regular postbag, together with a range of requests and queries from colleagues. Our advice with the post is that if it is addressed to you personally then open it, but if it is clearly a circular then don't bother. If, after you've been in post for about six months, you still get post for your predecessor then write back to correspondents asking them to remove your details from their mailing list. Letters from parents should be answered by return of post – even if it is only a holding response. Requests for information from colleagues should be prioritised as it can be very frustrating working with people who don't respond to requests. The adage 'if it's that urgent they will ask me again' is somewhat insulting to colleagues who have extra work to do when people don't respond to deadlines.

- *Plan for the future* – including the discussion of future events in the team meeting is a good way for the team to work together to prepare. By highlighting calendar points – for example report times – this gives everyone the opportunity to contribute and for the team to agree on how it will manage time.

- *On being a workaholic* – some people like to work very long hours and dedicate huge amounts of their personal time to their work. If this is you then feel good about it and enjoy what you are doing. Do the extra because you want to and because you enjoy doing it, and don't pretend otherwise. There is, however, a real difference between working very long hours because it's what you *want* to do and doing it because you feel *obliged* to, or because someone is making you do it. If you are oppressed by your work then it's important to talk to someone about it.

The job of being a teacher is certainly a demanding one and this is heightened by managing groups of people.

The business of managing your work–life balance is something that, given time, people can resolve. It is a personal matter because one person's cause of stress does not affect another in the same way. There are measures that can be taken to restore a work–life balance and these include:

- organising the agenda for meetings, starting on time and expecting people to prepare for the meeting, planning how long you will spend on each item and having a publicised end time

- planning your teaching so that you can take advantage of support staff to prepare materials for you

- setting aside time to undertake bigger tasks – for example department self-evaluation

- having at least one significant slot in the week dedicated to you, which is never cancelled nor eroded however busy the week – for example the Friday badminton club.

How well you are able to cope with the rigours of teaching and managing depends to a very great extent on how you maintain your focus on what is really important.

The passion that you bring to the task is another characteristic that helps you to transcend difficulty and enables you to find additional reserves of energy. The team in particular and schools in general need people who have a passion for what they do and who are able to bring energy, drive and resilience. It is easy to be positive when things are going well, but the strength you offer the team when something goes wrong will provide a greater learning experience than a succession of many positive days. Resolving issues to everyone's satisfaction is an important skill – one that your team expects you to do.

There will be occasions where things will go wrong and it may be because of what you did or said, or sometimes failed to do or say. Developing self-awareness and a willingness to listen and adapt is vital as you build your leadership and management skills and work with others.

Leading and managing a team should be great fun because it is about working with others and growing together to make improvements that benefit the children you teach.

Enjoy!

Index